Commercials, Just My Speed!!

Commercials, Just My Speed!!

by

Vernée Watson-Johnson

Wizards Production Group

Commercials, Just My Speed
Copyright © 1991, 1994 by Vernée Watson Johnson
First Edition 1991
Second Edition 1994

Library of Congress catalog card number 94-061198.
ISBN – 0-9639824-1-9

Illustrations by: Lorraine Hullum
Cover photograph by: Nancy Jo Gilchrist – Sherman Oaks, California
Published by: Wizards Production Group – P. O. Box 923252 – Sylmar, California 91392-3252

· About the Author ·

Vernée Watson Johnson is a native New Yorker who began her acting career at age 17 when she joined a theatre group. She attended New York University, majoring in Theatre Arts and continued her studies through private coaching. At age 19, she did her first national commercial which led to over 200 more and a Clio Award.

When Vernée migrated to the west coast, she landed a recurring role on *Welcome Back Kotter*, then series regular roles on *Carter Country* and *Foley Square* plus numerous guest starring appearances on shows like *The Love Boat, Fantasy Island, Benson, Hill St. Blues, The Jeffersons, Vegas, L.A. Law, Murphy Brown, A Different World, Married With Children*, and recurring as Will's mom on *The Fresh Prince of Bel-Air*. In addition, she's co-starred in movies such as *Norman, Is That You?, The Violation of Sarah McDavid, Death: By Reason of Insanity, The Boy in the Plastic Bubble, All Night Long, Showdown in Little Tokyo*, and the docu-drama *Angel Dust: The Wack Attack*, which won her an Emmy Award. Her talent extends to voice-overs in various animated cartoon series including *Captain Caveman, Scooby-Doo, The Flintstones, Batman*, and the voice of Danielle on *Baby Talk*.

In 1983 she married the man of her dreams, Van Elliott Johnson and they have two great kids, Sunde and Josh. She has owned and operated an acting school for children, coaches privately and continues to appear on TV commercials, sitcoms, episodics and films.

Vernée has enjoyed a very successful career and now shares this success through her books and videos.

ACKNOWLEDGEMENTS

Thank you Lord!

This book covers so many years and experiences that the list is long and includes family, and both personal and professional friends.

Special thanks to my husband, Van for his support and love and for giving me the idea in the first place. Thanks and kisses to my kids, Sunde and Josh, for being my inspiration and for making the writing of this book a real "live" experience.

Thanks to Ava for typing the first draft, Rosalind for typing the second, and Chris for typesetting and making it look like a book. Thanks to my proofreaders Adriane and Rhina. Thanks to Saundra Sharp for helping me to organize the information.

Individual "Thank you so much's" to my family: My mom, for being Mom and watching my kids, my Dad, my sister Brenda, my sister Lorraine, for her illustrations, my brother Walter, my husband's and my other Mom and Dad, Grand, Christell, Richard for helping me and Ava (well actually Ava) with the computer, Uncle Herbert, Aunt Nannie, Phil, Stephanie, Suzie, and the rest of my family for being the great people they are.

My dear supportive friends: Nikki & Kim, Rosie Lee & Robert, Ora, Candida, Tamu, Donna, Edward Love, Billy, Herb, Lorena, Pam, Martin, David, Gerry, Saul & Bernie, Francesca, Margarita (my hairstylist - cover), Juney, Gale, Linda, Shirley-Jo, Delbert, Eddie & Titi, Maureen (Mo) & Glenn, Marvin & Sheri, Larry & Linda, Larry Jacobs, and all my other friends who just wanted their name in my book – – a Big Thanks to You Too!

Thanks to my professional friends who helped me with information and interviews:

Agents Cindy Kazarian & Pamm Spencer at Kazarian/Spencer & Associates, actress Kim Bailey, actor Clyde Jones, director Mark Berndt, hair and make-up artist Joe DiMaggio, Don Pitts of Don Pitts Voices, and casting directors Beth Holmes and Megan Foley.

Finally, I would like to thank my instructors throughout the years: Otis Sallid, Maureen Samuels, Master Jesse Lechuga, Louise Bundy, Arthur Joseph, Thelma

Hill, Wynn Handman, Al Fann, Olympia Dukakis, Kristin Linklater, Lloyd Richards, Luigi, Roland Dupree, Hope Clark, Eleanor McCoy, Mini Gentry, and Ron O'Neal.

God Bless You All!

TABLE OF CONTENTS

Page

INTRODUCTION

At age 17, I got the acting bug when I joined a Harlem based theatre group called the Al Fann Theatrical Ensemble. I spent some long hours in class, did, probably over a hundred and fifty live performances, and then ventured out into TV land.

After I wore out quite a few pairs of shoes walking up and down Broadway, Madison Avenue, etc., knocking on doors and making contacts, I called upstairs. "Lord, I've paid some dues. I don't want to work long and hard. Let me do something that's quick but pays well."

He answered the last part but I still have to pay dues and work hard.

When I found out how much commercials pay and most of them shoot in one or two days, I said, "That's just my speed! I'm gonna learn how to do those." And I did. I never took a commercial class. I don't even think they had them back then, but I learned by doing.

You know the expression, "Knowledge comes from experience?" Well, at age 19, I filmed my first national commercial, and since then, along with sitcoms, episodics and films, I've done in excess of 200 commercials. One would assume that after 200 commercials, "the girl must know what she's doing." In some circles, I've even earned the title of "commercial queen."

Being the generous person that I am and a believer in giving back some of the good, I thought it would be nice to share the wealth of knowledge I've gained with those of you who are either embarking on a commercial career or have done a few, but not really broken any records.

This book is a combination of the techniques I've learned along the way, my personal experiences, and methods of developing your craft as an artist. Yes, I do believe that commercial acting is an art form as well as a business.

Although the finished product may look very natural and easy to attain, to the contrary, it is a tough competitive field and may require you to do and say things that are strange and unnatural but must look and sound "real."

There are several roads to commercial success. One being a short sweet journey when you're chosen right away because of your look, without having paid any dues or had much training. This happens to a few, but for most of us, the *road is long* and we must pay some serious dues along the way. This was certainly true in my case.

To make sure you don't miss a step I've broken the book up into three main sections:

HOW TO PREPARE

HOW TO GET THEM

and

HOW TO KEEP DOING THEM

with supplement sections on **VOICE, PRINT,** and **SURVIVAL TIPS.** In my early years as I prepared myself to be a professional actress I received training in a lot of different areas all related to the performing arts and most of which I have used and depended on in doing commercials. I have included these basics in the **HOW TO PREPARE** section.

This book is for the serious commercial actor who is interested in forming a strong foundation on which to build a long-lasting career. It is a home study program, with some invaluable tips that can turn into some valuable re$idual check$. So read carefully, study and get ready to work.

Chapter 1

As I mentioned in the introduction, the techniques I've learned as a performing artist have ended up to be some of the basic essentials I've needed as a commercial actress. *So prepare to help yourself, by doing some work on yourself.* This chapter deals with the basics of commercial acting, as well as, some fundamental techniques you need as a professional performer.

Back when I was in "acting boot camp" and getting my feet wet in television, I was told by people in the industry that I had a good commerical look. This meant then, and still does now, a kind of all-American, middle of the road, non-threatening look with the ability to turn on that bright healthy smile in an instant. I used this knowledge, decided to keep and capitalize on it, and have maintained a safe neat commercial look that works. So let's start with . . .

YOUR LOOK

Do you have that Commercial Look? Well that's a loaded question, because even though my look works, if you turn on your TV and observe some commercials, you realize that so does about a hundred other looks.

As far as I can decipher, the commercial look is based more on style and depends largely on what they're looking for.

A commercial director, Mark Berndt, once told me that a lot of times your ability to get a job depends mainly on your ability to read as a "type" in the first few seconds we see you on camera.

So let's review some of the *stereotypes* that are used in TV commercials and see where you can fit in or can adjust. I made the list according to age categories but it is in no way final, because in TV land they can come up with anything.

Verneé Watson-Johnson

Verneé Watson-Johnson

SOME OF MY COMMERCIAL
LOOKS THROUGHOUT THE YEARS

Vernée Watson

Vernée Watson Johnson

SOME OF MY COMMERCIAL LOOKS THROUGHOUT THE YEARS

As you review the lists, check off the ones you feel are in your realm.

CHILDREN

☐ Kid Next Door   ☐ Busy Body
☐ Hip Kid   ☐ Athlete (various sports)
☐ Nerd   ☐ Intellectual
☐ Dancer   ☐ Singer

TEENAGERS

☐ Kid Next Door   ☐ Student
☐ Intellectual   ☐ Athlete
☐ Counter person   ☐ Dancer
☐ Singer   ☐ Musician
☐ Rapper   ☐ Nerd
☐ Punk   ☐ Busy Body

YOUNG ADULTS

☐ Guy or Girl next door   ☐ Athlete
☐ College Student   ☐ Dancer
☐ Counter Person   ☐ Singer
☐ Musician   ☐ Young parent
☐ Blue collar worker   ☐ Yuppie
☐ Professional Career Person   ☐ Comedic
☐ Part of a couple

ADULTS

☐ Man or Lady next door   ☐ Teacher
☐ Parent, housewife, bachelor   ☐ Athlete
☐ Blue collar worker   ☐ Professional person
☐ Grandparents   ☐ Senior Citizen
☐ Comedic   ☐ Part of a couple

Speaking of types, it had gotten to a point where I was so well established, (and I'm not boasting, but commercials were and still are "my thang"), that they were asking for Vernée Watson types. Not me, mind you. They said I was overexposed, but they wanted my type. I thought this was pretty cool, even though I wasn't getting as much work, which is why I moved to California and started doing episodics too.

The categories I mentioned above are based on different character types. The following breakdown is based on appearance which, in most cases, is all you or your agent has to go on.

My agent has called and, aside from the time of the audition and product name, has said umpteen times, "They want nice casual," or "This is very casual" or "Go in upscale casual."

Nine out of ten times the call is for some degree of "casual". So let's take a look at what these terms mean and a few others that come up now and then.

•CASUAL

This area is also defined as *very real, down-playing* or even *ethnic*. Basically a very ordinary looking person. Wearing plain, simple wardrobe and hairstyle, and for females, little or no make-up. Be aware though, that this does not mean sloppy.

•NICE CASUAL

This means well groomed, attractive, neat but not too fancy. The attitude in this commercial look leans toward being very real, but safe. This is also called the P & G look, although recently the trend is a much more natural version of the P & G type. The majority of commercials are done in this category.

•UPSCALE CASUAL

Or just "upscale". This is a more dressy, classy look. This includes the career or professional person in an often non-professional situation. This look is attractive, well-groomed and professional looking make-up. Fluff up! Look clean, sharp and stylish.

•BUSINESS

This is a totally professional look, very well groomed and tailored with a professional business attitude. There is an air of confidence about this look and "upscale" that has to be there in the majority of situations. You may be able to attain this look but you must also be able to carry and sustain the professional attitude.

•HIGH FASHION

Those of you in this category usually know who you are; the beauties of nature, the stallions, creme of the crop. These people are usually very tall, extremely attractive, distinctive or exotic looking. This category cannot be faked as easily as some of the others. It's easier, if you are this type, to play yourself down and be more real, than if you are not, to grow five inches and become an instant beauty.

•CHARACTER

Thank goodness for this category because many people fit in here and do well. This area is wide open although there are certain character types that work more than others. If you do fall into this category, make sure to develop a workable look. Very ethnic or very radical looks also come under character, but they can be limiting.

Now take a look in a full length mirror and be honest with yourself. You can dress yourself up or down to get as many different looks as possible. Ladies, you can even consider a wig or two to change your look. (With wigs, it's better if you can blend in your own hair to make them look more natural).

Whatever look you develop, make sure you can attain it easily and can maintain it if needed.

YOUR PROFESSIONAL TOOLS

Along with your look, you also need to have in order your professional commercial tools: Wardrobe, Pictures, Resumé, Answering Service, etc. Since you're playing dress-up with your different looks, let's talk about the kinds of clothing that work best for commercials.

1. THE WORKABLE WARDROBE

Many commercial actors have what they call their "audition clothes". These are pieces used mainly for audition purposes and they are very special because they:

1. Range in look to cover the various types you would go up for.

2. Stay clean and ready to roll at a moments notice.

3. Can be balled up and stuffed in your bag if the need arises which it often does.

When things get rolling for you, you could have a call for three different looks in the same day and have a half hour to get ready. So with everything else you have to deal with, you don't need to worry about going to buy something, washing something out or ironing. In order to be cute by the time you get into each audition, the clothes you pick should give you the right look, sustain the packing and traveling and still look fresh.

Let's talk about the stuff that works and doesn't work. First of all, anytime you are given a specific request by your **agent**, or **casting director** always try to accomodate. One of the biggest complaints of casting directors is that actors do not come in dressed the part. So try to use what you have, be creative and honor their request as much as possible.

If you are not given specifics, here are some suggestions for the various looks.

WORKABLES

Generally these clothes should fit you well and be comfortable. Stick to warm colors that go well with your skin tone and a bright color here or there to bring you out a little.

•CASUAL

pair of jeans, cut-off jeans, shorts, (funky jeans only on request)
casual shorts, everyday slacks, plain skirt,
plain T-shirt, cotton or flannel casual shirt,
sweatshirt, vest, simple sweater, denim shirt,
tennis shoes or casual shoes,
a cap or cloth hat that doesn't cover your face, head scarf

•NICE CASUAL

The overall look for this one is generic middle America. In addition to some of the nicer looking pieces in your *casual* clothes, here are some suggestions:

tailored shirt/blouse
tailored slacks, 'Mommie looking skirt'
jogging suit
layered look
clean tennis shoes or loafer style shoe
sports outfit (when requested)

•UPSCALE

Still using some of your better slacks and skirts add:

a silk or dressy shirt/blouse
blazer or sports jacket
–OR–
pantsuit
neutral color good looking slacks or skirt
dressy sweater
nice scarf
smart looking, versatile vest

Remember you should be able to mix and match most of your wardrobe. Sometimes just a scarf or vest will pep up an outfit.

•BUSINESS

A couple of good tailored suits
Some tops used in upscale
Tie or pin
Tailored dress

•HIGH FASHION

Very stylish clothes that compliment your physique. They can be suggestive but not too revealing unless you're requested to do otherwise.

•COLORS

Stay in the warm neutral tones and pastels. Use bright colors but sparingly. Small prints or soft plaids.

•ACCESSORIES

Keep them very simple so they won't distract. Although your feet aren't usually seen on video your shoes should still compliment your overall look and not take away from it.

UNWORKABLES

Things to avoid:
Large prints
Solid white or solid black
Large/noisey jewelry
Dangling earrings
Clothes that are <u>too loud</u> or <u>too busy</u>

OPTIONALS

•GLASSES

If you wear glasses and you're not using them for your look or just to be able to see, ask if you should remove them.

•CONTACTS

No problem except I have seen people of color wearing contacts to match their outfit, whether it be green, blue, purple or yellow, etc. Color contacts are up to you but I suggest choosing a color that looks natural with your skin tone, because unless they ask for a unique look, casting directors prefer your natural eye color.

SUMMARY

All you need is a few good workable pieces to start and don't run out shopping first. Look in your closet and use some of that stuff you have already and add to it when necessary. Your *best choices* you can use for your next step which is *getting your first pictures*.

II. PICTURES

Your pictures are very important because they represent you and are usually your initial introduction to agents and casting directors. They are also what's left after you leave.

To start with, you need one good BLACK AND WHITE 8 X 10 head shot or 3/4 shot.

**WARNING:
CHEAP PHOTOGRAPHY IS HAZARDOUS TO YOUR CAREER!**

I went the cheap route once and the pictures on my *proofsheet* looked fine but when I got them blown up to 8 X 10 they were grainy, fuzzy, and out of focus. So, if need be, save up your ducats until you're able to make a good investment. My commercial agent Cindy says: "Don't go to a Joe Blow, $25 for 50 shots. It'll probably be 50 shots you can't use." They could be out of focus, badly lit, not framed correctly or just not the right look.

YOUR COMMERCIAL SHOT should:

1. **Be bright and animated** with lots of energy behind the eyes. "The look you want is energetic, with a wonderful smile and sparkling eyes. You want it to jump out at the casting director and say 'I can sell your product, hire me!'"

2. **Be complimentary**. You want to look good, not strange or silly. Even though you're putting life and energy into your picture you still want to be very <u>NATURAL</u>.

3. **Be positive and act as your calling card**. As we said earlier, it is usually the first thing an agent or casting director sees of you and what is left to REPRESENT YOU when you leave, so you want to make a positive impression.

4. **LOOK LIKE YOU** are going to look for awhile. Don't spend a few hundred bucks on pictures and then the next month change your look by cutting your hair, blowing up your lips, chiseling your nose or growing a beard, etc.

   Technically, your 8 X 10 should always:

5. **BE IN FOCUS** – a sharp picture.

6. **BE WELL FRAMED** – you should be in the center of the picture without too much busy background.

7. **HAVE NICE TONES** – not too contrasty with a soft background that doesn't distract.

If you don't already have an agent, your 8 x 10 is used in getting one so it's important to have the best picture possible. Once you get an agent, they may ask you to update your pictures. They used to require a composite with a headshot on the front and (4) four different looks on the back, but more recently it has been simplified to (2) two 8 x 10 shots.

One on the front;

– generic, all American guy or girl next door, mom/dads

One on the back;

– character, business or comedic look

(see example pg. 13 – 14)

Or you could just use one good commercial looking shot with a resumé on the back. (see pg. 15 – 15A, 16 – 16A)

Once you get an agent, your pictures are used on submissions to casting directors. They act as your calling card and take note though that standards are always changing. Your agency will advise you on the type of pictures they prefer but to get going an 8 x 10 headshot or 3/4 shot will do.

•MAKEUP FOR PICTURES

REAL AND NATURAL LOOKING. Unless you're going for the high fashion look, keep it simple with light shadings and definition. For guys, you may need just a consistently lightly applied base and some powder but:

I STRONGLY RECOMMEND A PROFESSIONAL MAKE-UP ARTIST who has done commercial shots before.

Vernée Watson Johnson

MIKE JAMES

MIKE JAMES

SAG-AFTRA

TELEVISION

IN LIVING COLOR	Featured	Paul Miller, Director
FLASH	Co-Star	Jonathan Sanger, Director
MANCUSO, FBI	Featured	Roy Campanella II, Director
YOUNG AND THE RESTLESS	Guest Star	CBS
FREDDY'S NIGHTMARES	Featured	Dwight Little, Director
WHO'S THE BOSS	Guest Star	Asaad Kelada, Director
NURSE BOB	Featured	NBC-Pilot
L.A. LAW	Featured	Kim Friedman, Director

FILM

STONE COLD	Featured	Craig Baxley, Director
THE CHAMPION	"Best Actor-Italian TV Film Fest"	Mini-Series, New Zealand
SECOND SON	"Winner of 11 Film Short Awards"	Charles Evans Jr. Prod.
HEAD GEAR	Co-Star	American Film Institute
NO WAY OUT	Featured	Orion Pictures
CRACK	Lead	American Film Institute
THRILLER		Optimum Productions
NO MEANS NO: DATE RAPE	Lead	Shriller Productions

THEATRE

1ST BREEZE OF SUMMER	Nathan	The Globe Theatre
A RAISIN IN THE SUN	Walter Lee	Morgan-Wixson Theatre
A SOLDIER'S PLAY	C.J. Memphis	Morgan-Wixson Theatre
NIGHTSIDE	Leonard	International City Theatre
GLASSHOUSE	Tony	Wilshire Ebell Theatre
STREAMERS	Roger	Fig Tree Theatre
A LOSS OF ROSES	Kenny	Camino Theatre
WHAT THE WINE SELLERS BUY	Rico	Camino Theatre
STREAMERS	Carlyle	Caminito Theatre

COMMERCIALS & VOICE-OVERS: List Upon Request

TRAINING:

ACTING: Uta Hagen-Herbert Berghof Studio, New York
Michael Holmes
Robert Spera's Audition Lab
L.A.C.C. Academy Theatre

COMEDY: Bill Hudnut's Sitcom Workshop

COMMERCIALS: Estelle Tepper

SPECIAL SKILLS: All Major Sports, Track and Field, Racquetball, Dancing, Singing, Songwriting, West Indies Dialect and Street Jargon

Kimberly Bailey

Joseph
Heldfond &
Rix, Inc.

1717 N. Highland Ave., L.A., CA 90028
213/466-9111 • FAX 213/466-3352
A KAZARIAN-SPENCER-PITTS CO.

Kimberly Bailey

SAG/AFTRA

HEIGHT: 5'5"
WEIGHT: 120
COLOR HAIR: Black
COLOR EYES: Brown

FILM:	ROLE	DIRECTOR
This Dancing Life	Lena Murphy	Juney Smith
Good to Go	Marsha	Juney Smith
The Nation	Betsy	Juney Smith
For Keeps	Baby Cakes	John Avildsen

TELEVISION		
Nerds III (MOW)	Co-Star	Roland Medina
She Stood Alone (MOW)	Starring	Jack Gold
Quantum Leap	Guest Star	Michael Vejar
A Different World	Guest Star	Ellen Falcon
Highway to Heaven	Guest Star	Michael Landon
New Gidget	Guest Star	Roger Duchowny
What's Happening Now	Guest Star	M. Neema Barnette
The Judge	Guest Star	Kip Walton
Superior Court	Guest Star	Joe Bahar

COMMERCIALS: UPON REQUEST

THEATER: PARTIAL LIST

PLAY		
For Colored Girls ...	Lady in Brown	Harman Avenue Theatre
Jonin'	Sheila	Harman Avenue Theatre
Glasshouse	April	Embassy/Ebony Theatre
One Flew Over the Cuckoo's Nest	Billie	Haunted Theatre
Greased, Fried & Laid to the Side	Greta Gucci	Groundlings Theatre
South of Where We Live	Edwina	Theatre of the Arts
Love and Other Four Letter Words	Edna/Artisha	Inglewood Playhouse
Last of the Red Hot Lovers	Elaine	Stardust Studios
An Anthem to Black Artistry	Toussaint	The Ensemble Studio
Moon on a Rainbow Shawl	Esther	Rainbow Connections
Five on the Black Hand Side	Gail	Rainbow Connections
Livin Fat	Candy	Rainbow Connections
The Me Nobody Knows	Melba	Tacoma Actors Guild

SPECIAL SKILLS

Voice-overs, Cooking, Swimming, Bicycling, Sewing, Horseback Riding and Sign Language.

TRAINING

Vernee Watson-Johnson (Acting Coach)
Rainbow Connections - Los Angeles, CA
Al Fann Theatrical Ensemble (Commercial Training) - Los Angeles, CA

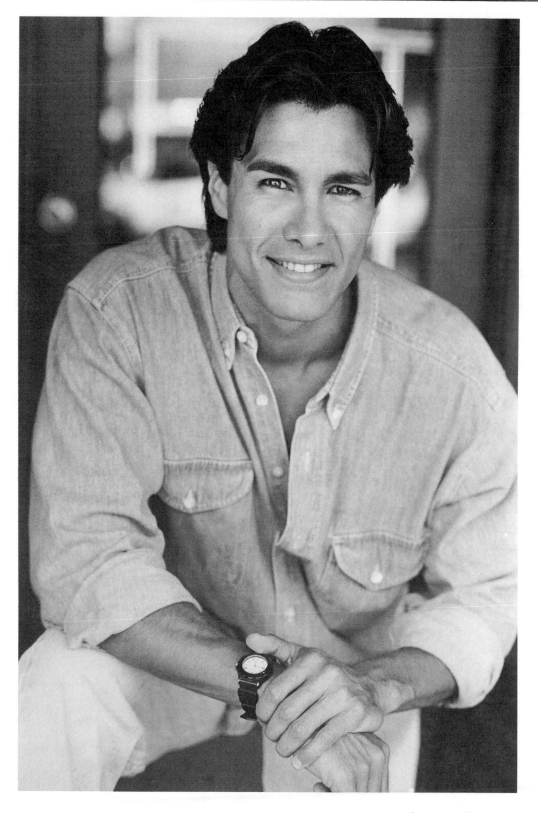

Rick Julian

•HAIR

NEAT AND STYLISH BUT NOTHING TOO DRASTIC. Remember you're dealing with TV land and we don't want to scare them. The strange look doesn't sell as well.

I ALSO RECOMMEND A PROFESSIONAL HAIR STYLIST or get a makeup artist who does both.

•WARDROBE

NICE CASUAL is best. Of course if you're doing 2 different looks you'll need two changes, but bring plenty of choices and use what works best.

•OPTIONS

If you wear **GLASSES** it is not necessary to wear them in your pictures unless it is the "look" you're after or, later on, you and your agent decide to use them for your other look.

FACIAL HAIR is not usually recommended but if that's your "thang", try it.

TOUCH-UPS –go lightly on the air brushing, if at all. Remember they're going to see you too, and there's nothing worse than having an overly touched-up picture so that you're not recognizable when you walk through the door.

CHOOSING A PHOTOGRAPHER

If you want to get the <u>BEST</u> person for the least amount of money, you have to shop around. Ask your friends for references or an agent can refer you to a photographer once you've signed with them. Also the <u>TRADE papers</u> are full of photographer advertisements. When you choose a few, call and set an appointment for an INTERVIEW first.

• **THE INTERVIEW**

LOOK THROUGH THE PHOTOGRAPHER'S BOOK to see:

- the quality of their work

- the type of people they've photographed; have they done your "type",

    people with your skin tone

- do they capture the commercial look

CHECK OUT THE ENVIRONMENT

Is it comfortable for you

Do you feel safe, at ease

If you wish, ask, if they will provide music

If smoke bothers you, make sure they're non-smokers

• **LIGHTING**

Is it studio lighting or are they just going to use natural light which means mostly outside shots?

• **PRICE**

FOR THE SESSION AND FOR PRINTS. What does the price include?

• **HAIR – MAKEUP – WARDROBE**

Do they furnish any or all

Are they included in the price

How much additional

See samples of their work

If they provide wardrobe, see if it works for you.

Remember you only need **BLACK & WHITE**.

PICTURE OF CONTACT SHEET

•THE SESSION

Be well rested and well groomed.

Plan to be early

Plan or prepare a lunch if it's going to be a long day, but generally it only takes a few hours.

Take along your FAVORITE MUSIC, RELAX, HAVE FUN, THINK POSITIVE THOUGHTS.

• PROOFSHEETS

A few days after the session the photographer will give you *proofsheets* or *contact sheets*. They'll contain all the pictures from the session. From those you choose which ones to get enlarged to 8 x 10 prints. If you already have an agent then they should have a say in your decision since they know what kind of pictures work and what casting directors are looking for.

Don't go crazy ordering 10 or 15 prints if you had a great session. Narrow it down to a few shots with different looks. If you have a bad session just print one or two and see what you've got.

• REPRODUCTIONS

Get a referral or check the trades for a place that does 8 x 10's repros. The one or two shots you've chosen to reproduce, get at least 50 copies of each.

Your REPROS should

–   have your name printed on the front

–   be of good quality paper

–   closely resemble the print in tone and contrast.

(Ask to see a test before copies are run off).

Once you get an agent <u>always</u> keep them supplied with pictures. They can't work for you unless you give them something to work with.

• NEGATIVES

KEEP TRACK OF ALL YOUR NEGATIVES. Know where they are and how to get a hold of them so you can get more copies done quickly when you need them.

• UPDATING

Even after you get that perfect 8 x 10 there will always come a time to update and get new pictures. You and your agent will decide when that is. Usually when you've...

> Changed your image with a new look, hairdo, etc.

> Gotten a little older

> Decided to try a new category

So be prepared and save up for the event.

III. RESUMES

A resumé, attached to the back of your picture can be used in getting an agent and once you do, your agent then uses both on submissions. In today's competitive market more and more casting directors are asking for resumés. Even if you have not had much experience, you should put together a professional looking resumé that includes the following: name, contact number, height, weight, SS#, hair and eye color, union affiliation, special skills and training. Of course if you have done films or TV shows be sure and list them, each separately, and any plays you've been in list them under theatre.

However, DO NOT list commercials. Just state – "Commercial upon

Request" or "Commercial Tape Available."

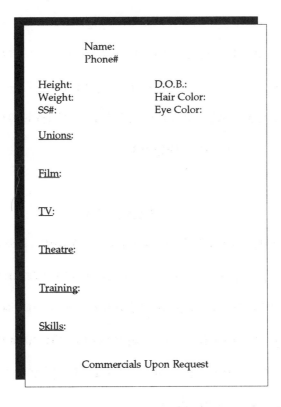

IV. ANSWERING SERVICE

This is a <u>must</u>. Have an answering machine, a voice mail or beeper where you can receive a message and **check it often**. It's pretty frustrating to miss out because you didn't check your service.

V. COMMERCIAL TAPE

(optional but a great idea)

Once you start doing commercials, get copies of them from the advertising agencies and put them together on a tape or reel. You and your agent can use this reel to show producers and clients upon request.

YOUR PERSONAL TOOLS

Most people want to get some pictures and run out and get an agent. Well... a good agent will only want to represent you if they feel you are ready to work and can go out and get the job. So while you're getting your look, your wardrobe, and your money together to get some good pictures, let's get you personal tools sharpened and learn some basic acting techniques.

WARM-UPS

As a commercial talent and coach, I've always found it best to begin with physical and vocal warm-ups. If your body and voice aren't working properly, neither will you. Aside from helping to keep yourself in tune, in shape and ready, these warm-ups are a great way of relieving stress and tension before performing. So for the next few pages I'll take you through some basic physical warm-up techniques followed by some work on your voice.

• FACE

An expressive face is a big plus in commercial acting, so let's loosen up and wake up the face.

Start by tightening all the muscles in your face. Shut your eyes tight, squeeze your lips together and pinch your face together as tight as you can. Hold for ten counts while exhaling.

Now, shake it out –– loosely shaking the head from side to side letting all the facial muscles go very loose, blowing out through the lips.

Then repeat the exercise.

This may not look pretty, but it sure wakes up the face and gives you a healthy glow. It also helps keep your face toned for that youthful look.

• CHEEKS, MOUTH AND CHIN

In a chewing, churning motion, rotate the cheeks and lips to the front several times then rotate to the back several times keeping tension in the lips and cheeks.

Now release by blowing loosely through the lips. Now rotate cheeks and lips to the right then left and release.

You should do all these exercises until the muscles in your face get tired. Soon you will feel and see a firmer face that looks more alive and healthy.

• EYES

We need our eyes so much but seldom do we think about exercising them. By strengthening the muscles in and around your eyes, you may also strengthen your eyesight. In commercial acting we need good vision to read copy, storyboards and to hit marks.

I have a theory about eyes and aging, When we are young we look at something, give it our full attention, and see it clearly. Those times when we would daydream (not focusing) someone would usualy snap us out of it.

As we get older, the daydreaming turns into worrying, concern or just thinking about something other than what we're looking at. Then, when we want to focus, we have to readjust our eyes and concentrate. We get out of the habit of just living moment to moment and simply seeing what we're looking at, so our eyes get fuzzy. We start trying to adjust our focus by moving the object further away or closer to see, read or write. So, be aware, as you go through your daily life, try to focus on what you're looking at, even if you have to think about some-

thing else.

1.   Looking straight ahead, squint the muscles around the eyes together, then release. You should feel the muscles under the eyes and in the eyelids tightening up. Repeat several times.

2.   Holding the head straight and still, focus on a spot to the extreme right and then to the extreme left. Repeat several times.

3.   Keeping the head straight and still, focus on a spot as far up as possible then as far down as possible. Repeat.

4.   Now the four corners. Keeping the head still, focus on the farthest four points that you can see making a square. Hit those four points to the right several times, then to the left. (Move to these points slowly at first until you can spot them easily. Then speed it up)

5.   Now circle the eyes around the room going right then left, several times each way.

Now relax. Close your eyes and rub the palms of your hands together until they're warm, and cup the eyes with your hands. Take deep breaths, inhaling through the nose, exhaling through the mouth.

• **NECK AND SHOULDERS**

The following exercises help to relieve tension and stretch out the muscles.

Standing up straight, hands behind you, the left hand holding the right wrist, keeping chest high, tilt head to the left, pull arm down and stretch. Change directions – – tilt head to right, right hand holding left wrist pull the left shoulder down and stretch the neck over to the right. Repeat both sides. Drop head forward. Drop it back. Forward, back, rotate, roll head around slowly to right, roll to the left slowly – – stretching the neck and pressing the shoulders down.

•ARMS AND HANDS

1. Circle arms to the front, then the back and repeat several times.

2. Arms out to the sides, rotate just the hands to the front, then the back and repeat several times.

3. Arms down, elbows out a little to side, rotate both shoulders to the front several times then rotate to the back. Squeeze shoulders up, then press them down and repeat.

Now release and shake out hands and arms vigorously.

• WAIST, BACK AND BACK OF LEGS

1. Spread your feet about three feet apart, turn them out, keep your body facing front. Stretch the left arm over toward the right, reaching for the wall, bounce gently for 8 counts. Stretch to left side, right arm over reach and bounce eight counts to the left.

2. To the back – – First turn the feet parallel (straight forward) and release the head to the back, leaning back as far as possible while bouncing gently for eight counts. Keep your hands out front for balance.

3. Now bend over forward, both hands touching the floor if possible, bounce gently eight counts, knees as straight as possible. Roll up slowly for eight counts and repeat the exercise.

• LEGS, HIPS

This is my favorite. It's hard, but it's so good. Okay, starting with feet spread about three feet apart as above (so you can go right into this after the side stretch), you are going to do deep knee bends in second position, knees turned out. Press out over your feet (toe and heel) pressing through the floor as you come up. Keep toes spread out, arms go up over the head, hands together as you go down, then they circle down, hands together pointing to the floor as you come up. (The same movement as you use when doing jumping jacks). Once again, go down, bending knees (keeping knees turned out), go as far down as possible below knee level. Now press up, straightening knees, pushing feet through floor. Don't forget to breathe and repeat 'til you can't take it no mo'. Shake out legs and arms. If you do these faithfully, you'll be surprised how firm and toned you'll get.

<u>Squeeze and Release</u>

Now squeeze up, and tighten every muscle in your body. Squeeze your face, shoulders (pulling down), make fists, squeeze derriere, legs and knees tight, tight, crunch up your toes, hold several counts. Then release and stretch it all out. On your toes, arms up and reaching out to the furthest point, mouth stretched open, eyes wide, tongue out as far as possible -- hold several counts then shake it all out. Shake the head loosely, face muscle slack, arms and legs so loose you could "throw them away". Shake out, very freely, then take a deep breath in, arms come up, push the breath out, arms lower then repeat the exercise.

You should be feeling pretty good by now. For additional body toning and stretching that I've used through the years, check my **survival tips** in the supplement section.

Let's move on to our Voices.

<u>VOICE</u>

You can be all dressed up, looking cute, your face bright and alive, but if your voice is weak and inaudible, it's all for naught. Commercial auditioning can be very nerve racking. How often have you opened your mouth to speak, in a tense situation, and your voice cracked? This section will help remedy that problem.

In order to gain voice control and be able to project and sustain as an actor, you have got to know how to properly use your **diaphragm**. *It is the center of your energy and the power behind your voice.* Strengthening your diaphragm and speaking from that central area gives you more control of your sound, and helps control hoarseness even in stressful situations.

Being able to regulate the flow of air from this area will help you handle commercials with lots of dialogue.

Okay, so what is the Diaphragm?

As seen in the diagram below, the diaphragm is the horizontal muscle right under the lungs that goes down to let the air into the lungs and goes up to push air out.

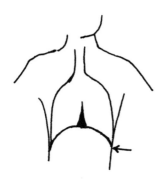

(A partition of muscle separating the chest and abdominal cavities) The diaphragm is the center of your energy.

Think of the lungs as two balloons. As you put air in, they expand and as you let air out, they deflate. As you pull air in, expand the diaphragm filling up way down in the stomach first, then expand the back, then fill up the chest last. As you release, you pull in slowly and steadily with your stomach muscles which push the diaphragm up pushing the air up and out of the lungs at an even flow. YOU DO NOT COLLAPSE THE CHEST. The chest stays lifted while the diaphragm and stomach muscles work.

As you let the air escape out on an even flow, bring it up through the roof of the mouth but in a straight line, pulling the stomach all the way in, slowly. Feel your energy aiming up and out from your center.

Throughout the following exercises keep a loose jaw with your throat as loose and open as possible. Speaking from a tense throat is very dangerous and is a misuse of the larynx and vocal chords.

EXERCISES TO STRENGTHEN THE DIAPHRAGM

Because this area is so important, I'm giving you five different vocal exercises to do for general vocal strength and especially as a warm-up before an audition or commercial job.

These will require a little knowledge of music, so if you could get access to a piano, pitch pipe or recorder, it would help. However, if you can hit a note in your head and you're able to go up a step, down a step, or run through the octave, then you don't need an instrument.

In commercial acting, the lower tones of your voice are for a more sophisticated or sexy sound. Middle tones are the announcer or everyday person. Upper levels are for a brighter, more animated, even comedic sound.

So you should work the full range of your voice in these exercises.

Remember to fill up all the way, chest high, shoulders relaxed. Let the sound and air come out through the roof of the mouth through a loose relaxed jaw. Keep your hand on your stomach so that as you inhale, you can feel the stomach expand and as you exhale, the stomach pulls in slowly.

HEY

Down and up the scale holding on the high notes and the low note. Make sure you fill up and in one breath on a nice full 'Hey' sound, Slide (descending) down to the low note. Hold. Slide (ascending) up to the high note. Hold. The exercise is done *(legato)*, meaning it is done smoothly with one note flowing into the other. If you don't have a piano, start on a note around the same pitch as your normal speaking voice. If you do have one, start on middle C then go down the octave and back up to middle C. Take a breath, fill up, start again on Hey, one step up to D. Down the octave, then back up to D.

These exercises are written in the bass clef because I want you to start in the low tones and ascend throughout the exercise.

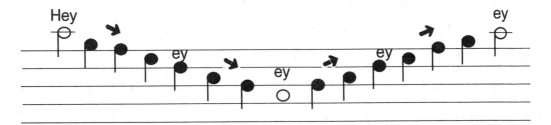

Keep going up one step at a time until your voice reaches its limit. Then start at C again and go down one step at a time to the bottom limit.

If you're working from your diaphragm and keeping a nice loose jaw, the Hey should come out full and rich with a lot of volume behind it. If it sounds weak and shaky, drop the jaw more and try to keep the image of the balloon. As you fill it up, it expands, as the air and sound come out, it deflates (stomach goes in). If you're running out of air, you may either have not taken enough in, let too much out on the 'H' sound, or you're not pulling the stomach in enough toward end.

HUM

Do the same scales as the exercise before but only this time, to feel your voice placement, close your mouth and hum. Starting on top, holding, slide down the octave, hold, then back up to the top. Hold. If your lips are closed but soft and you're bringing the air up through the roof of your mouth (even though in this case, out the nose), you should feel a tickle in the lips and a vibration in your nose and face. Keep your hand on your stomach to make sure you're working correctly.

B-R-R-R

Using the same scales as the first two exercises, blow the air through loose lips giving you a B-R-R-R sound. Descend the octave on B-R-R-R then back up holding the last note. Repeat going one step up each time as high as you can go. This one really works not only the diaphragm, but warms up the lips. It tickles the nose too!

HEY HEY, HI HI, HEY OVER THERE, HI OVER THERE

This exercise is a little different, but it is fun. It combines (staccato) and (legato). Staccato means you don't hold the note. You hit it quickly with lots of energy then you get off of it. This is good for the diaphragm because between each and every note in staccato you let the air drop in quickly and on the note you push out quickly so the stomach is moving in and out rapidly and getting a good workout.

Now I said this one is a combination. So the first notes are staccato (HEY HEY HI HI), and the last notes are legato (HEY OVER THERE, HI OVER THERE).

Here's some imagery: Imagine yourself high on top of a mountain peak calling to someone on the mountain peak across the valley.

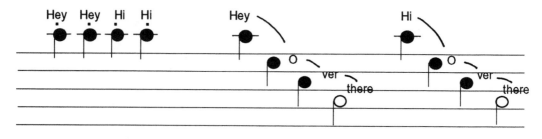

You start with a C major chord, then go the the D major, E major and so on. Putting hand on stomach and taking a breath between each, push out. HEY HEY HI HI (hit them – let them go). Now smoothly (legato) descending the chord:

HEY O-VER THERE (Holding THERE)

HI O-VER THERE (Hold as long as possible)

If you don't have a piano you hit HEY, go down three steps to "O", two steps to "VER", then two steps to "THERE".

"HEY" Being The Top Note of Octave

"THERE" Being The Bottom of Octave

HEY HEE HI HO HOO's (Like A, E, I, O, U)

This is the ultimate diaphragm workout. It may seem complicated but follow along and between the words and music, you'll get the idea. You do one vowel sound at a time with the H in front. They're done quickly, all staccato except the last note.

Going up the scale starting on C (an octave below middle C) skip up a step, go back a step, skip up a step, go back a step, skip up a step, go back a step, skip up a step, go back a step, skip down a step, up a step, skip down a step, down a step, stay and hold. The last note you hold the longest.

Then, still on HEY, start on middle C going basically in one direction this time. C, skip down a step, up a step, skip down a step, up a step, skip down a step, up a step, skip down a step, up a step, skip down a step, up a step, down a step, down a step, stay, Hold. Stop.

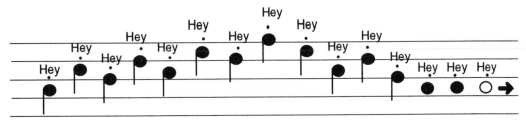

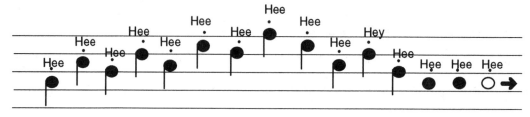

Make sure you're keeping your hand on your stomach to feel it work quickly in and out. Just release out to let the air in and pull in to push the sound out only holding, pulling, all the way in on the very last note.

Now do the same on **HEE**, then **HI**, etc. Then raise the pitch to D, then E, etc. Do as much as you can adding more the next time.

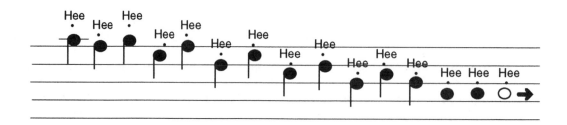

Okay. The voice and diaphragm should be humming by now. If your throat is a little tired just relax it, roll the head and drink some water or hot tea and lemon, but if you're working correctly you should not be hoarse.

THE SPEAKING VOICE

Many of us have a lazy tongue or are just not used to articulating and clearly annunciating every syllable, which is required in most commercial copy. Your dialogue in a commercial may have taken months to be written and approved, so each word is important.

Once, on a commercial shoot for *NUT N' HONEY* cereal, the child I was working with had trouble pronouncing the product name. Even though Nut N' Honey is grammatically incorrect, it had to be said so that it comes out clearly. The child would swallow the words and the director and client were getting frustrated. I pulled the child aside and explained to him that there were four syllables in "Nut N' Hon-ey" and that his little tongue and lips had to work so that the words would come out clear and correct. He found that with a "conscious effort" he was able to do it.

That's a simple example, but you will run into copy that is much more complicated.

So let's work on our speaking voice.

Still using the diaphragm, fill all the way up speaking slowly but say as much as you can before taking another breath. Really working the lips and tongue, pronouncing every vowel, every consonant, the beginning and end of each word, try these fun tongue twisters:

During these exercises use a tape recorder to record your voice and listen to the playback carefully. Circle your trouble spots with a pencil and work on them. Only erase the circles when you have corrected that spot.

On a typical spring day,
one might say
The callalillies are in bloom
This is the best time of May.

Say it slowly making sure you pronounce the beginning and end of each word.

Try these:

Archibold Agarway arched his eyebrows with an axe.
Arched his eyebrows with an axe did Archibold Argarway.
If Archibold Argarway arched his eyebrows with an axe,
Where is the axe that Archibold Argarway arched his eyebrows with?

Read it so that it makes sense, taking pauses where you see the comma's. Break

the unfamiliar words up so that you say them correctly with all the syllables.

Catherine Certanapy caught a quimsical quirk.
A quimsical quirk did Catherine Certanapy catch.
If Catherine Certanapy caught a quimsical quirk,
Where's the quimisical quirk, Catherine Certanapy caught?

Donald Dutchmire dumped his dog in the ditch.
Dumped his dog in the ditch did Donald Dutchmire.
If Donald Dutchmire dumped his dog in the ditch,
Where's the ditch in which Donald Dutchmire dumped his dog?

* Make sure you pronounce the p's and d's.

Francis Funkleroy fought a fantastic feat.
A fantastic feat did Francis Funkleroy fight.
If Francis Funkleroy fought a fantastic feat,
Where's the feat that Francis Funkleroy fought?

Grandia Grant grunted and groaned for grapes.
Grunted and groaned for grapes, did Grandia Grant.
If Grandia Grant grunted and groaned for grapes.
Where are the grapes for which Grandia Grant grunted and groaned.

Do these very dramatically and have fun with them. Do them slowly with lots of

energy, using the mountain peak image we used in "Hey Over There". Or do them

crisp and quickly like a schoolteacher or a newscaster. Even try them with different

accents that you are familiar with.

ACCENTS

If you have a regional accent, this is the time to work on controlling it to the point that it is not distinctive. You can always call upon your accent if the situation calls for it or if you are asked to sound more ethnic. But generally you should develop a crisp, clean manner of speaking that is unidentifiable to a certain region or culture and that is friendly, warm and pleasant to listen to.

The most used commercial sound is that of middle America: a clear articulate voice that you can color with expression but is always controlled.

PRACTICE IN READING COPY

Let's move on to reading some commercial material.

Pick up a magazine and find a commercial advertisement with lots of dialogue. These are great to use because there's such a variety of them, and from working on them you get a sense of how commercials are written.

Warm-up your lips with the B-R-R-R-R exercises because first we want to make sure the lips and tongue are working correctly to pronounce all the sounds, vowels and consonants.

Now, read out loud using your diaphragm, going very slowly at first, exaggerating the mouth movements, pronouncing each syllable, making sure each vowel and consonant in each syllable is distinct. We must work on getting rid of the lazy mouth and tongue. The only way is to work them very consciously. In this exercise, the first time you read the ad is strictly for enunciation. The second time through, circle or underline the words or phrases you have trouble with, even if you just stumble a little. If you're having a problem pronouncing a syllable within a word, circle that word as you go through. Once you've gone through the second time, noting your mistakes, take the time to break down each and every trouble spot. Figure out what your lips and tongue should be doing and practice saying it over and over until your mouth gets used to it and you can say it easily. Now read the entire sentence that the trouble spot was in and see if you have made the correction. If so, move on to the next one, working it over and over until it's comfortable and you're sure you've made the correction.

Now read the copy again at a normal speed and hear how good you sound. If you're doing it correctly, you should hear a difference and realize you've just helped yourself quite a bit.

If the ad you've chosen is easy for you, find one that gives you a challenge.

INTERPRETATION

So, you have some practice copy, you can pronounce all the words but you certainly don't want to sound like you're reading. How many times have you heard so called actors who sound just like that? Bad news.

Being able to interpret the material and read it so that it sounds natural and conversational is a very important technique in commerical acting.

Instead of just reading sentences, pay close attention to the punctuation and define the thought behind each phrase. Read through with more expression this time, trying to reveal the thoughts behind the words. Connect those thoughts that should be connected and make smooth transitions in changes of thought patterns. Work on finding different levels in your voice, being all the time, aware of your articulation, but adding your imagination and personality.

The next time you read, it should sound as if you're carrying on a conversation. It should be clear, interesting, and flow very naturally. After using this method of practicing for some time, you will get used to taking unfamiliar copy and making it your own in shorter periods of time. However, no matter how familiar you become with this exercise, you should continue to work on it throughout your career to keep your tools sharp.

• PICKING A CHARACTER

In commercial acting you have to be able to instantly come up with a character, taking on a certain attitude and behavior, or becoming a completely different person in a matter of seconds.

To add more realism to the interpretation of your materials, choose a character that best fits each situation. Try to pick ads with variety and range so that you can work different characters.

To develop a character ask yourself some questions. Your work on your character should coincide with the facts and relationship in the commercial and involves specific and believable answers to basically six questions in every situation.

1. **Who** are you: i.e., business person, mom, dad, customer, etc.

2. **What** do you want: your objective in this situation i.e., you want relief, you want something to eat, drink, etc.

3. **Why:** your motivation or reason for saying what you're saying.

4. **How** do you feel: about what you're doing or saying.

5. **Where** does this take place?

6. **When** does this take place?

These are basic questions for character and situation development.

However, in commerical acting, usually time does not allow for such a deep analysis. So, any amount of time you put into character development on your own, is time well spent because it enables you to make intelligent, creative and natural choices quickly.

DELIVERY

The next step is to relate the material to camera or whomever you're speaking to. So let's work on our delivery technique.

If you have a video camera and can record yourself during these exercises, by all means do so. If you don't have one, mark a spot on the wall in front of you with tape like "<>" or "X". Let it be at least 3" in diameter.

The object is to be able to read and absorb enough so that you can look away from the paper and face into the camera, your mark on the wall, or wherever you're directed to look. Then continue to glance down for the next phrase or sentence capturing the thought and delivering it up and out and so on.

If you've been working on the copy for awhile you should be familiar enough with it that this technique comes easily. You may even have it memorized.

Find new ads to work on too so that you can (1) practice instantly absorbing phrases and delivering them to camera; (2) practice a variety of attitudes, thought patterns, and words; (3) develop your cold-reading skills (see page 41 on Cold Readings)

MEMORIZATION

It's easier to memorize lines by memorizing the thought patterns behind the lines first. Once you know what your character is thinking, it's easier to recall what he or she is saying.

Standing or sitting, hold the copy down and away from you so that you can refer to it, but it is not covering the upper third of your body. Focus on your camera spot and see how much you can deliver without referring to the paper.

Whatever spots you had trouble with, go back over that section several times, glancing at your copy connecting the thoughts and words to what proceeds it and what comes after it until the thoughts flow correctly for you. If you have trouble connecting the end of one sentence to the beginning of another just repeat the end and the beginning a few times until it clicks.

Work the ad through like this connecting thought to thought, sentence to sentence until you have completely memorized it. Or you can become so familiar with it and the placement of the words on the page that even if you get stuck in your delivery, your eyes can quickly glance down, put you right back on track, and go back to focusing into camera.

The more you work the technique with different material the better your memorization skills will become. The more familiar you are with the copy the more you can make it your own.

COLD READINGS

A cold reading is when you are handed a piece of copy and asked to instantly <u>read it</u>, <u>make sense out of it</u>, <u>and deliver it</u>, without time to warm up or look it over.

<u>**Instant Interpretation, Characterization and Delivery**</u>.

Most of the time, in auditioning, you'll have a few minutes to review the copy but not always.

In commercial acting you may do cold readings:

1. during an interview with an agent

2. during auditions:

     where copy isn't available until you get into the audition room,

– OR –

when there are changes once you get into the room.

All the work you do on Interpretation, Delivery and Memorization <u>help</u> when it comes to cold readings.

Cold reading basics:

1. the ability to read and absorb each phrase quickly

2. making smooth transitions – connecting the thoughts and phrases

3. delivery – relating your material to the camera or person you're speaking to.

So when you're asked to do a cold reading, as you go along, quickly read and absorb each phrase and deliver it up and out with as much thought and interpretation as possible.

PANTOMIME

Another element of commercial auditioning is working with objects that aren't really there. This is called <u>pantomime</u>.

Using objects that aren't physically there, but through your sense of recall you recreate their presence. We have all done some degree of pantomime. For instance, when we pretend to be drinking something or combing our hair or writing, we demonstrate the activity without having the object. In commercial acting, if you don't use pantomime correctly, it can become distracting and confusing. Take for example, you're supposed to be eating cereal with a spoon and then passing the box of cereal to someone else. If you don't have a real sense of the spoon and box, the spoon can disappear when you go to reach for the box or your hand could go through the box, or you're pretending to eat food and it doesn't really look like you're putting the food in your mouth. The director could imagine that the food was all over your face and the table. To help us avoid such instances and learn the art of pantomime, let's start with the main rule.

Each action of pantomime has a Beginning, a Middle, and an End.

The Beginning is your first contact with the object; picking it up, lifting it, holding it, and/or moving it.

The Middle is the way the object fits into your hand, the texture, the weight, the consistency, the way the object is moved by your hand; what the fingers are doing, the space between them, the amount of tension in your hand from holding the object.

The End is your release of the object, putting it down and/or letting it go, passing it over, throwing it away or eating it.

If your pantomime involves eating something, this has it's own beginning, middle, and end – – separate – – but coming out of the action of getting the food.

The Beginning is the bite.

The Middle is tasting and chewing the food.

The End is swallowing the food.

Recalling all the components of the action involving an object is called sense memory. We are going to use our sense memory to do pantomime in some exercises. Remember to pay close attention to the Beginning, Middle and End of the action. Stay relaxed so that your senses can work to their fullest, and don't hold any tension in the hands unless it's necessary. Focus on what you're doing, using your senses of sight, sound, smell, and touch. First, use the real objects in the action and then put them aside and do the action again using your sense memory.

Here are some we're familiar with, (notice the differences in the actions):

1.   Drinking a glass of water, or bottle of juice.

2.   Combing your hair, brushing your hair.

3.   Writing a note.

4.   Reading a paper, book, magazine (notice the different sizes and ways of turning the pages).

If you have to use several props or sets make sure your props are the same size when you pantomime and your sets are at the same level or height, for instance, a table top or counter.

It's hard to pantomime sitting in a chair and usually it's not necessary. Here are more involved activities.

5.   Eating a hot dog, hamburger, piece of chicken, salad, cereal, or spaghetti. These are all very different and remember also, picking up the food and eating are two different activities. I suggest that you first do these looking in a mirror. Be very careful not to exaggerate your movements. Pantomime should look very real and natural. Don't overdo it because you're acting.

6.   Putting on and taking off clothes. Start with one article, then use several. Make sure the pieces of clothing don't disappear in your hands.

7.   Peeling an apple. This one is good because your hands are doing several things at once, all in sync. Rotating the apple in one hand and the thumb of the other hand pushing it around while peeling it too. Make sure your hands keep the roundness of the apple.

8.   Serving dinner.

9.   Making a sandwich.

10. Fixing a bike.

11. Building something.

12. Washing dishes.

13. Driving a car.

14. Riding a bus.

15. Riding an elevator.

16. Pulling a rop (tug-of-war).

The last few exercises fall under the category of *mime* which involves the entire body reacting to movement, force, or space. These are very important also because, often in auditioning we are asked to react to a given environment or create an environment and activity.

For instance: being in the cold or heat, a crowded space, in the rain, or in a moving car or bus. The best way to develop a sense memory about them is to actually experience them. As you go through your daily life become more aware of your body language and your surroundings. Notice how your muscles react instinctively to certain conditions or changes. When you have a chance, recreate the experience in pantomime or mime to broaden and sharpen your sense memory.

Aside from the actions I suggested, I'm sure you can discover many more exercises in pantomime and mime that may end up being just the thing you needed in an audition. Remember, in mime the action also has a Beginning, Middle, and End.

The Beginning – start of the action, getting on the bus, stepping out into the cold, etc.

The Middle – your body's reaction to the movement of the bus (remember, if you grab something to hold onto, that's a separate pantomime within the mime), your body's reaction to the cold or heat or force – – as in tug-of-war, or being pushed or blown by the wind.

The End – your coming to the end of the action or resolving it, i.e., getting off the bus, coming out of the cold, letting go of the rope.

Here's an exercise *in moving through space* that can help with changes in the environment.

SPACE EXERCISE

1.   Clear an area for yourself where you can walk around freely and not bump into anything. We start with a light environment, changing slowly to a heavy atmosphere back to light. Walk around the room. Imagine the surrounding air

being very light with a nice warm breeze blowing, very easy to move through and very comfortable. It begins to get a little misty and cloudy. Now the air is getting thick with no breeze and it's not as easy to move through or to breathe. It begins to get very stuffy, thick, dirty, and hot (like L.A. smog or N.Y. humidity). You are extremely uncomfortable. Finally, it begins to let up a little (very little at first). There is a little movement in the air, and your breathing is getting easier. It's getting clearer and clearer and a breeze is beginning to blow more and cool you off. Finally, the air has lightened up again and you can move freely and feel much better.

2.   Now do the same exercise and instead of the air going from light and warm to thick and hot, it goes from light and warm to thick and cold. It gets so cold and heavy that you can hardly move and in the freezing air, it hurts to breathe. From this extreme it begins to ease up slowly and get a little warmer as your body loosens up a little until you are completely comfortable and moving freely.

The main thing in this exercise is to go through it very slowly and to really feel the changes in your space.

These are just a few examples of the pantomime and mime actions you may be asked to do, but at least you have a good basis and understanding of how they're done.

IMPROVISATION / CREATIVE DIALOGUE

Some auditions have no written copy at all and you may have to make up your own. So, apart from being able to create space, you may and should be able to create your own dialogue in a given situation. For practice, make up a situation where you're telling someone a story. Using the past tense and a lot of imagination, just start talking and keep going. For instance: "I was walking along the street one day and I ran into an old friend I hadn't seen in years. We were so surprised so see each other. We just stood there with our mouths open and finally we hugged. Then the stories began. I told her about..." It can go on and on.

–OR–

"You won't believe what happened to me yesterday..." Or anything else you come up with as long as you keep it going.

Now change to present or future tense. For instance:

"Today is such a busy day. I have three auditions to go to and each one is a different look. The first one is..."

–OR–

"I know exactly what I'm going to do to get the ball rolling..."

The dialogue can begin in hundreds of different ways and can lead to hundreds of different places, but being able to create it on the spot takes practice and the more you work at it, guess what, the better you'll get.

STAGE DIRECTION versus CAMERA DIRECTION

You need to know the areas of the stage so that you'll know in which direction to move.

Once you begin to audition and work, you will be given direction to move according to the eye of the camera which is the opposite of the stage. So let's figure it out.

1.   The performers point of view as they face the camera or audience:

Back wall of stage or performing area

Upstage Right	Upstage Center	Upstage Left
Center Stage Right	Center Stage	Center Stage Left
Down Stage Right	Down Stage Center	Down Stage Left

Camera

Audience

2.   Camera point of view:

Away from Camera	
Camera Left	Camera Right
Toward Camera	

Camera

Audience

These terms are used in theatre, film, TV, and commercial acting, so learn them and their differences.

Notice that *camera right* or *left* is the direct opposite of *stage right* and *left*.

Some commercial directors will say "your right or left" instead of "stage right or left".

Note that from the camera's point of view it's "toward" and "away" from camera, instead of "down" and "up".

To practice these, set up your area, call the positions off randomly and move to those points or in that direction until you get the hang of it.

YOUR PERFORMANCE

Let's put all the things we've learned so far together. Pick several different commercials that you've worked on with variety in:

Amounts of dialogue,

Character types

and settings

Think of your commercials as little performances which are actually what they are in auditions or shootings. So, let's bring your commercials up to performance level.

Create a set for each commercial making it as real as possible using your own environment. Costume yourself and create a good commercial look for your character. Use real or substitute props, pantomime or mime where you can, and a set with minimal furnishings.

Work through your commercial, determining each thought behind each line and being aware of your transitions. Give yourself stage directions and movements but confine them to a small area. Try performing at different levels of intensity.

Each time you do them, something should be a little different as you discover more about your character and the copy.

So have fun with them. Let your imagination go and your creative juices flow.

AN AGENT

An agent/agency acts as your representative in the commercial industry. When you sign with an agency, both parties sign standard union contracts from the Screens Actors Guild (SAG) and AFTRA. Basically, it states that they will represent you commercially (send you on auditions, negotiate your deals, and sell you as a client), in exchange for 10% of your gross income of the jobs you booked through them. **They are working for you. You are working for yourself and with them**.

You can only sign with one commercial agent at a time. However, in some cities you don't have to sign but you can be registered with several who send you out according to who gets the call first.

The agent receives breakdowns from commercial casting directors (CD's) or producers, describing the type or types they need for a particular spot.

If it's your category, the agent submits your picture along with others in your category and if you're one of the ones chosen by the CD, you get a call from your agent for an audition, (which is a trial performance), to see if you're right for the job.

Generally, you will not be called to audition unless you're submitted by an agent.

Methods haven't changed much in getting that first agent from when I got mine.

1. I got a list of franchised agents from a theatrical book store.

2. I mailed or hand delivered my headshot and resume (such as it was) to a good number of agents I chose from the list (maybe thirty or forty).

3. I followed up with phone calls or visits trying to set up appointments with those who were interested.

4. They interviewed me. I interviewed them and made my choice.

GETTING AN AGENT

1. **Get a list of union franchised agencies from a theatrical bookstore that includes information on:**

   a. type of agency

   b. who works in the different departments

   c. what type they represent

Some lists also give information about sending in pictures/calling/general auditions, etc.

Each agency is set up differently. Some of them have departments that cover other areas of the commercial industry in which you may be interested. For example, print, voice, theatrical, dance, directing, and others.

Choose the ones you think will fit your needs and make sure they are SAG franchised agencies.

2. **Do mailings**

   Send out a headshot and resume (with basic information if nothing else) to the ones you've chosen.

*A young actress by the name of Kimberly Bailey who had done a couple of plays in Washington came out to Los Angeles, took acting classes, and had a lot of desire to build a career. What she did was get a hundred copies made of her headshot, a meager but professional looking resume, and went to Samuel French Bookstore, and got a copy of a book containing all the **agents franchised under S.A.G.** (The book is entitled, The Agencies, and has about 200 listings). After carefully reviewing it she picked out seventy-five agencies. Out of the seventy-five, she sent pictures to half of them (in case the first half yielded a quick response, she could* *save her pictures). She got several replies from her first mailing and set up interviews with two of them. After meeting with both agencies, gettting a feel for each and information about their setups she decided on one which has worked out very well for her for several years.*

3. **Follow-up**

   by calling or stopping by to:

   a. Set up an interview

   b. Attend a general audition or an open call

Note: Don't call the ones that say "No Calls". They'll call you if they're interested.

4. **Interview them when they interview you. Find out:**

   a. How their set-up works.

   b. How many others they represent in your category. They may have too many like you already. (In any case, you'll still have to compete with many more of your peers from other agencies at auditions, so if they don't mind, go for it or choose another agency).

   You may be asked:

   a. about previous experience – (don't lie, you may get caught)

   b. age – your true age, basically for "Truth of Advertising" purposes where legally you must be a certain age. i.e. a beer commercial, beauty ad where you state your age.

   c. about training you've had and current training

   d. about hobbies and special interests

   e. to do a cold reading of commercial copy

f. to do a monologue

g. if you have any tape on yourself

(People who have done commercials already and are looking for a new agent may be asked for a commercial tape. Otherwise, if you have a good looking class tape or demo tape to give them an idea of how you look on camera, offer it to them).

Most top agencies want to see a tape on you but it is not the decision maker. 'Look' and 'Personality' are.

WHEN YOU FIRST SIGN WITH AN AGENT

You should set out to have a cooperative relationship, getting to know everyone in the office and their function.

You should sign a union contract, not an individual agency contract. Your first contract is for one year with an 'out' clause written into it. Basically, you have a good year to decide whether you have made the right choice, and you should remain with them only if you feel they have represented you properly.

I have been fortunate enough to be with the same agency for fifteen years to date. They're a top agency on the west coast and my ladies, Pamm and Cindy, have given me some other tips on getting that first agent.

OTHER METHODS OF GETTING AN AGENT

1. Referrals

The easiest way is through a referral of someone who is with an agent and is willing to recommend you.

If you have decided to go with a manager *(see glossary)* first, he or she can refer you to an agency.

Casting Directors

You can do mailings to CD's, a list can be obtained at a SAG office. Do the follow-ups and find out when they will have their next **general** or **open audition**. After the audition, if they are impressed with you they can refer you, or...

Some Casting Directors have commercial acting classes. If you take their classes and they feel you're ready and know you need an agent, they may give you a referral.

If you want to make personal contact by stopping by and leaving your picture and resume, don't be pushy but be specific about introducing yourself and asking about open auditions. Often times you cannot see the CD's themselves, but an assistant will help you. The best calling card is a notice about a play you're doing that you wish to invite them to, and always be sure to offer them complimentary tickets.

2. **Plays**

Agents agree that theatre training is an excellent basis for all acting and good theatre is an excellent showcase for your talent.

You may do a lot of plays but not all of them are good representations of your work. Be patient, get in a good production, then showcase yourself, inviting agents and/or casting directors.

You can be in a play and make contact with an agent someone else invited, who sees your work, is impressed and expresses an interest in you.

Doing good work has many benefits, so always be at your best.

Now, after you get an agent, you will then begin to audition. So, let's move on...

Chapter 2

HOW TO
GET THEM

PART 1

•HOW LONG WILL IT TAKE?

My students always ask me, "How long will it take before I get my first job?" And I say, "Well, I tell you... I went on twenty auditions before I got my first job. It was a national commercial for *Pampers* with my friend, Hope Clarke. We were sisters and we both had babies that drove us nuts. But it was my start and after that I would win some and lose some.

There have been times when I was really HOT! My friends, (who would also happen to be in my category) would see me coming in auditions and say, 'Oh, L-a-w-d! here she comes.' Then to me 'What are you doin' here? Aren't you working enough already? Let somebody else get a job.

And then... there are times when, as my friend Saundra would say, 'I can't get arrested!' But if I only shoot two commercials in a year, and they're good running national spots, the residuals are so nice, I'm set for a good while.

You have to sow so many seeds in order for any of them to sprout. You keep planting and those bookings will start sprouting here and there.

It's the "Law of Averages", and your average will fluctuate throughout the year.

•HOW MUCH WILL I MAKE?

That depends on:

- What TYPE of commercial it is: National Network, Regional, Wildspot, Dealer, Cable.
- Where the commercial is airing -- i.e. New York only, Southeast only, all across the U.S., etc.
- How many times it plays

Your agent will usually tell you what type you're going up for. Information on TYPES and USAGE is detailed and explained in the SAG Commercial Contract Manual along with all you need to know about payments, contracts, work laws, etc.

I will say that a good running national spot could pay well into the five digits.

For now, my business is to help you get them. So, let's prepare ourselves for the auditioning process.

AUDITIONING

I don't know anyone who books every job they go up for. But the more you go on, the better. You can only become adept at auditioning by doing them.

It's to your benefit to GET AS MUCH EXPERIENCE AT AUDITIONING AS POSSIBLE.

•WHAT IS IT?

An audition, also known as an *interview* or *a call* is a trial performance to determine whether or not the performer is right for the job.

It takes place at a casting session and is usually videotaped to be reviewed by the director and the clients.

You could be asked to do <u>almost anything</u> in <u>almost no time</u> at all <u>AND</u> even though it is a trial performance, it should be <u>done well</u> if you intend to get the job.

You should discuss with your agent the type of calls you will be submitted for, the age range and categories, many of which we have listed in Part One. Of course, there can always be something different or unusual that you will be called upon to do, but for the general areas of submission you should be prepared to take on the different looks for the different categories.

•TOO MUCH OF A GOOD THING?

There have been times when I've had three auditions in the same day, with three different looks, in three different parts of town. By the time the third call came in I would have the nerve to get an attitude because of all the running around I'd have to do. But I had to learn to organize and be prepared as much as possible and <u>be glad</u> I had three chances at getting a job in one day.

Because this business can be so crazy and uncertain, it's best to be as ready as possible so...

GET READY

Audition clothes: keep your audition clothes that we talked about in "Workable Wardrobe" ready to go. If you have to carry changes, if possible, just add to or take from your basic outfit for your different looks.

<u>To make changes</u> you can usually use the restrooms or even a dressing room in some studios. <u>Leave yourself enough time</u> and don't forget the accessories, i.e., socks, stockings, ties, slips, belts, etc.

Audition Make-up/Grooming. We've already discussed a natural looking make-up for your pictures and the same holds true for auditions.

If you have to dress up your look for another audition bring along extra eye-shadows and liners.

Keep <u>the shine down</u> with face powder or tissue in case you've heated up on the way to the audition.

Keep <u>the lips moist</u> (for guys, too) watch out for chapped lips.

Keep <u>the hair groomed</u> – take a comb and a brush for wild or wind blown hairs that show up so well on video.

Keep <u>the eyes clear</u> – keep some gentle and safe eye drops on hand for bloodshot eyes.

Keep <u>the nails clean</u> – and manicured. They often ask to see your hands. If you wear polish, stay in the neutral tones.

•HELPFUL HINTS:

Pack a lunch. If you have to run all day, make sure to eat before you leave, if possible (not just coffee), and make yourself a sandwich or take along some fruit to recharge during the day. This also keeps you from eating junk or having to go out of your way to find a decent snack.

Bring a bottle of water. Your body needs more water than you know. Having some fresh water available to you and drinking it throughout the day helps keep everything flowing in the right direction. Sometimes you may feel a little weak, queasy, sluggish, or have a little headache, and all you need is a good intake of water to bounce you right back again. It also helps to freshen up your mouth and clear your throat right before an audition. Beware, drinking water also causes you to use the restroom more, so make the rest stops whenever you can and don't try to hold it because it may take longer than you expected to get to your next destination and you don't need that discomfort.

•WAKE-UP AND WARM-UP:

Do your facial and vocal warm-ups on the way. To tone the lips and tongue and work your diction, recite something or read signs aloud on the way. ***Caution: If you're driving, keep your eyes on the road and just glance at signs, as you would a traffic sign, then back to the road.***

Quick glances help with cold readings.

GET SET

• Invest in a date book and write your appointments in it <u>first</u> instead of on little pieces of paper which you can easily lose. Keep your datebook by the phone with a working pen or pencil in it so that you will be ready when your agent calls.

• Have a <u>dependable means of transportation</u> and try not to rely on others.

• Work out conflicts! You cannot be in two places at once, so don't try it just because you don't want to miss something. You should always want to be calm and at your best, so work out any conflicts with your agent and give yourself enough time between appointments to allow for traffic, parking, changing and/or just calming down.

If you're going to be late, let your agent know so they can call ahead. Take the stress off of yourself.

Get all the information you possibly can concerning each audition. Make sure you get the correct time, date, place, product, and casting director.

•KNOW WHERE YOU'RE GOING:

If the address of the audition is unfamiliar to you, ask your agent what it's near, or better still, get a Thomas Guide and look it up so you'll know exactly where you're going and how to get there. If you have more than one audition, you should plan your route between them, keeping in mind traffic, distance, and parking time, especially if they're scheduled close together. As you go along, make yourself familiar with the parking conditions and regulations in the surrounding areas. This can give you more options and save you money in parking tickets as well as time in finding a spot. Also make sure you have plenty of coin change for parking meters. Those of us using public transportation, especially in Los Angeles, (New

York is not such a problem, just the traffic), check the schedules and make sure you can make the connections.

• KNOW WHAT THEY'RE LOOKING FOR:

Get as much information as possible about the type they're looking for, age range, and any available character descriptions. Type, in this instance, may be casual, nice casual, upscale, high fashion, business, or whatever else they come up with. Character description means the role you would play: student, mom, dad, teacher, worker, secretary, executive, or whomever. Sometimes they even have information on attitude or tone being used in the commercial, for instance, *lots of excitement, very serious, comedic, animated, very real, natural, or straight on.*

Find out if there is any copy (dialogue) and how much. Sometimes your agent will tell you there is no copy, they're just "looking for a look". In these cases, the descriptive information is most important. Other times they'll say no dialogue, just reactions, which we'll talk about soon, but be prepared to listen to directions and not just make faces. Then there's the improvisation audition where you create your own dialogue so the creative juices need to be flowing. If there is copy, your agent may not know how much, but there are times when they'll say 'lots of copy' so prepare to get there early so that you have ample time to work on it. We will be discussing these variations in auditioning and doing copy breakdown a little later on in this chapter, but right now it's...

LA AUDITION – – GO FOR IT!

Okay, you have arrived at the audition. What do you do first?

Well, as you can imagine, I've been on quite a few of them and most of the time I run into people I know. So the first thing that usually happens is a lot of "Hey, Girl, how you doin'? I ain't seen you since the last one", etc. It's like old home week (a term we use).

Now it's okay to say "hi" to your friends but over the years I've learned to minimize it and take care of <u>business first</u>.

Another danger in socializing is the noise level which interferes with the actual audition process going on in the studio. In having a good time, you may be embarrassed by a casting director telling you to be quiet, which is not a good way to start off.

So be **QUIET, POLITE** and **TAKE CARE OF BUSINESS FIRST**.

1. **Find out which studio your commercial is being cast in**. Most casting houses have a number of studios and as you enter, the studio numbers and commercial titles are posted. Find yours and go to that studio waiting area. Several things can happen next. If you have to change for this audition go do that first. If you're ready and just need to freshen up and there are several people ahead of you, then:

2. **Sign in**. The CD provides a sign-in sheet on which you write your name (legibly), and give other information which I'll explain soon. Make sure you sign in on the correct one. The product name should be written on the top. An example is on page 63.

3. **Get the copy**. Check the storyboard. If there's copy, take one and look it over. There may also be a *storyboard* (see glossary) or other information concerning the commercial. Look all of it over. If there's more than one person in the spot, and your agent has not yet advised you, find out from the casting person as soon as one is available, which one you will be reading and who you will be reading with. Quite often the casting person is in the audition room and comes out intermittently. There may also be some other instructions or directions they wish to give you, so be aware.

4. **Fill out the <u>size sheet</u>**. This needs to be done most of the time and you are either told to do so, or it is posted. An explanation of the size sheet starts on page 64.

5. **Wait and Work on The Copy**.

   Go over it and over it until you have it down. If you have a partner or partners, work with them. When you're satisfied with your performance then you can relax until you go in. If it's a long wait and you've decided to do a little socializing, make sure you go back to the copy before you go in.

6. Also, while you're sitting in the waiting area and noticing other actors, here's a good piece of advice from casting director, Beth Holmes, "Don't play casting director". In other words, don't sit there and type yourself out and say, "I must not be right for this" based on other types you may see. I'll say it again. You never know what they're looking for or what the casting director has in mind. **(Don't dwell on negative thoughts.) (Keep yourself positive with a professional attitude.)**

   If you feel yourself becoming agitated because of the long wait, don't take it personally, and remember this often happens. If you're going to go in the audition room carrying an attitude from having to wait, you might as well go home. On a positive note, if you've waited this long, you should be even more determined to get the job by being professional, making a good impression and performing well.

   Also be aware that often when you do have a time problem (meaning you need to leave at a certain time in order to make another appointment), you can make the casting director aware and hopefully they would try and work it out for you.

Explanation of the Sign-In Sheet

<table>
<tr>
<td colspan="2">

COMMERCIAL PERFORMERS:
► Print your name.
► Print agent's name.
► Circle applicable interview.

</td>
<td colspan="3" align="center">

EXHIBIT E
SAG / AFTRA
COMMERCIAL AUDITION REPORT

</td>
<td colspan="2">

THIS FORM MUST BE FILLED OUT IN INK
PAGE_____ OF_____

</td>
</tr>
</table>

TO BE COMPLETED BY CASTING DIRECTOR

(X) WHERE APPLICABLE   TELEVISION ☐   ON CAMERA ☐   OFF CAMERA ☐   RADIO ☐   AUDITION DATE

INTENDED USE   UNION: SAG ☐ AFTRA ☐   Person to whom correspondence concerning this form shall be sent: (Name & Phone Number)

CASTING REPRESENTATIVE NAME   COMMERICAL TITLE - NAME & NUMBER   ADVERTISER NAME

PRODUCT   JOB NUMBER   ADVERTISING AGENCY AND CITY   PRODUCTION COMPANY

INSTRUCTIONS: Circle the name of performer hired if known.   Mail one copy to SAG OR AFTRA on the 1st and 15th of each month.

TO BE COMPLETED BY PERFORMERS

NAME (PLEASE PRINT)	SOCIAL SECURITY NUMBER	AGENT (PLEASE PRINT)	ACTUAL CALL	TIME IN	TIME OUT	INITIAL	CIRCLE INTERVIEW NUMBER	SEX (X) M	F	AGE (X) +40	-40	ETHNICITY (X) AP	B	C	LH	I	PWD (X)
							1st 2nd 3rd 4th										
							1st 2nd 3rd 4th										
							1st 2nd 3rd 4th										
							1st 2nd 3rd 4th										
							1st 2nd 3rd 4th										
							1st 2nd 3rd 4th										
							1st 2nd 3rd 4th										
							1st 2nd 3rd 4th										
							1st 2nd 3rd 4th										
							1st 2nd 3rd 4th										
							1st 2nd 3rd 4th										
							1st 2nd 3rd 4th										
							1st 2nd 3rd 4th										
							1st 2nd 3rd 4th										

This recorded audition material will not be used as a client demo, an audience reaction commercial, for copy testing or as a scratch track without payment of the minimum compensation provided for in the Commercials Contract and shall be used solely to determine the suitability of the performer for a specific commercial.
AUTHORIZED REPRESENTATIVE SIGNATURE_____

The only reason for requesting information on ethnicity, sex, age, and disability is for the talent unions to monitor applicant flow. The furnishing of such information is on a VOLUNTARY basis. The Authorized Representative's signature on this form shall not constitute a verification of the information supplied by performers.

Asian/Pacific — AP   Latino/Hispanic — L
Black — B   Native American — I
Caucasian — C   Performer with Disability — PWD

28 EXE / 8

This is how they look. You print your name, social security number, agent, time of call, time you arrived, sex, age group and ethnicity. If the sheet is full or you don't see one, ask the CD or an assistant for one. Upon leaving, be sure to SIGN OUT. If the audition has run overtime and you have been there over an hour, you are entitled to compensation. The hour begins at your call time, even if you're early, or when you sign in, if you're late, and ends when you sign out.

A casting director can use the sign-in sheet to call you in to audition, or they can go by a list they have with your name and call time. Usually when they use a separate list, they have you paired with someone, or in a particular group.

SIZE SHEET OR CASTING SHEET

The size sheet is used for <u>call backs</u>, matching up pairs, groups, families, and also by the production company for wardrobing and other information if you get the commercial. They come in different shapes and sizes, but the information needed is generally the same. Make a strong effort to fill out as much information as possible to make things easier if you get the job, and be as honest and accurate as possible. Giving wrong information out of embarrassment or any other reason just wastes valuable time. As told to me by director Mark Berndt, "When you book a job, there is usually very little time between the booking, being confirmed, and the production company being able to contact you, shop for you, and wardrobe you for the commercial. Giving the right information can save a lot of time and hassle."

Be sure that your handwriting is legible. If the person trying to get information cannot read your handwriting, it can be irritating. An idea of what they look like is on the following page. Others may need additional information. Get out your measuring tape if you're not sure of your measurements, and make a note of it in your datebook. Also memorize your agents phone number since you always need it.

Product _____   **SIZE SHEET**

date _____

name _____

home address _____

_____   _____   _____   _____
city   zip   home phone   ans. service

agent _____   agent phone _____

age _____ weight _____ height _____ hair _____ eyes _____

Work Permit (if under 18 yrs.) ☐ Yes   ☐ No

measurements _____ ss# _____

jacket _____ dress _____ shirt/blouse _____

waist _____ inseam _____ shoes _____

hat _____ glove _____

SAG _____ AFTRA _____ AFM _____ AGVA _____

Special Skills:

_____

_____

_____

POLAROID

Will you work as an extra?
☐ Yes   ☐ No

Some of it is self explanatory, but let's go through it anyway.

Product	=	Product you're being seen for.
Date	=	Today's date
Name	=	Your professional name. If it's the same as your real name, just write that. A parent filling this out for a child should write the child's name and give the child's information.
Home Address	=	The Production Co. would use this if they needed to send you something or pick up something.
SSN	=	Social Security Number – This is the second time you've needed this so far so be sure you know it. You can also use it for I-9 identification (after you get the job) if you have your card with you. So you should carry it, or a copy of it, and keep it in a safe place. Parents, also have your child's SS# and card handy.
Agent	=	The name of your agency. Make sure you put your commercial agent, not theatrical if you have one. Often you need their phone number.
Four Unions	=	Check the ones that you are a member of. Be sure to keep your union dues up to date. It could cause you big problems and you can't work if you're not in good standing with your union (paid up). If you do work, and you're not paid up, the client will be fined and all concerned will be very unhappy. So keep your dues current and parents keep your child's work permit current.

NAMES OF UNIONS
SAG –Screen Actors Guild
AFTRA –American Federation of Television and Radio Artists

> AFTRA is an open union. One year after joining AFTRA, you are eligible to join SAG.

AFM–American Federation of Musicians
AGVA–American Guild of Variety Artists

Age	=	In a commercial where 'Truth of Advertising' is required which means legally you must be a certain age to do the commercial, put your exact true age. Otherwise, if you don't want to put your real age, use your age range or age group. If they have a problem with it they will ask you to be specific. Parents must give their child's real age because of the labor laws for different ages.
Eyes	=	Your true eye color. Please beware of those colored contacts. Many of them look fake and very strange with some different skin tones. If you must have some color contacts, get some that look natural and relatively normal for your skin tone and ethnicity.

Height	=	Unless you're going for high fashion, there really isn't a need for you to be extra tall. So be honest. They may have to match you with someone and you may not be able or want to wear those lifts or 4" heels all day.
Weight	=	The camera may put a few pounds on, but it surely doesn't take 10-15 lbs. off, so give them as accurate an answer as possible. They need this information to get an idea of your body frame. If you have a problem, then work on it and get your weight down, or build up if such is the case.
Hair	=	Hair color is especially important for specifics they may have in their clients' request, matching up families, and other reasons, so be specific and always let your agent know about any change in your hair color. Hair length and texture is not necesary unless it's for some hair product and more detailed info is needed.
Hands	=	Good, Fair, or Bad. They need to know if your hands are in good enough condition to be shot close up. Your hands are an important element in the commercials. They often ask you to hold them up while they're taping you and take a close-up look at them. So if not in model-perfect condition, at least keep them in good condition. People with especially pretty hands can do hand modeling. Get or give yourself manicures, and use hand lotion.
Measurements	=	Give your current sizes. If you don't have some of this information like glove and hat size, don't panic just fill out what you have. When you learn the others, use them so they'll stay familiar to you.
Suit	=	Your suit size. If your size fluctuates between two sizes according to the cut, then put both. Guys be sure you put R (regular) or L (long).
Waist	=	Waist size. I wouldn't advise putting the smallest possible number. You don't want to be uncomfortable if they have to fit you with something. Remember, you have to wear it all day, eat lunch, and chances are you can't loosen it because the shot has to match.
Glove	=	Not many people know this information, and it's not often needed but you never know when it can pop up, so find out your glove size and make a note of it in your datebook.
Dress	=	Ladies, don't try to be cute because you never know what the cut is going to be. If you have to give yourself leeway, then put two sizes.
Hat	=	They might put one of these on you at any time so know your size even if its small, medium or large.
Inseam	=	The number of inches from the crotch to the point where your pants would end. This is important for men as well as women

since they often dress women in slacks.

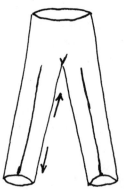

Shirt	=	Shirt size for guys. Blouse size for girls.
Shoes	=	If you have ever had your feet hurt from shoes being too small, you know this information is nothing to lie about. Think comfort.
Hobbies	=	If you have any hobbies that you're really into, mention them, especially if you feel they relate to the product or type they're casting. There is no need to make up things just to fill it in. You might be called on it and be embarrassed.
Special Skills	=	If you truly have special skills, list them. If you know the commercial calls for a special skill and you are adept at it, put it down. But it can be most embarrassing and often very dangerous if you say you can do something and you really can't. Don't put yourself in jeopardy just to get the job. There will be others and if you lie, the consequences can be many and unnecessary. So think about what your real talents are or are not, and be honest about it.
Will you work as an extra?	=	Talk to your agent about this. Although extra work is good experience for beginners, you don't want to become known as solely an extra player.

Well, that's the size sheet more or less except the section that says polaroid.

• POLAROID (Photo)

This space is for the polaroid snapshot that they take of you at the audition. These are a joke in the business and they usually come out looking pretty bad, but they say you're not cast from them. All you can do is freshen up, give a nice smile and don't worry about it. Spend that energy working on the copy.

• THE COPY

In working on your copy, if you have any questions, ask the CD or an assistant who's available to clarify it for you.

If there's more than one part sometimes they're interchangeable and you will be asked to do several different roles, so know the copy.

If storyboards are posted, look them over and see what your actions are, especially any action with the product. Try to correlate the dialogue with the action as shown on the storyboard as much as you can. If you're having trouble, don't worry about it because it's all usually explained to you by the casting director, and specific directions are given in the audition room. Even then, they may change, so your main focus should be on the dialogue.

• WORKING ON IT

Don't be shy about reading your copy aloud. Find a spot or just stay where you are and focus. Quietly read through it articulating and enunciating all the words properly. If you have any questions as to how a word is pronounced, especially the product name, ask questions and get the correct pronunciation. Just as you did in your cold reading exercises, as you read through copy and come across a word or phrase that gives you trouble, work on it using your lips and tongue correctly until you work it out and the words flow smoothly. It is always good to also say the words or phrases before and after the trouble spot so that you become secure in knowing that it will come out correctly in context and not just by itself. On some copy, the dialogue will be on one half of the page and scene description and directions on the other half. Make sure you read them over to get a sense of what is happening in the scene and what your specific directions are. There may even be a storyboard posted in the waiting area that shows what is going on in the spot and hints as to what the camera shots will be.

• COPY BREAKDOWN

The time you have to work on copy at an audition is limited, so the following would be a quick mental process. But for practice and to get used to breaking down copy to help you understand what's going on, here are some points.

1. Decide what the overall thoughts are behind the spot; what point are they trying to make; what method of selling are they using?

2. What do they want the consumer to feel or know about the product? What are the descriptive words or phrases?

3. Are there any transitions or changes in thought or emotion? Do they evolve out of another thought and emotion, are they reactions or are they spontaneous?

4. What are the points of comparison?

5. What are the benefits being brought out?

6. Are there any points of conflict or objections being made?

We'll do more work on copy breakdown later in the chapter.

• MEMORIZING

Try to commit the copy to memory as you go. The more familiar you are with the material the better you will be able to perform it.

Just as you did in Chapter One, on "How To Prepare", apply the same techniques here.

– Connecting thoughts and phrases instead of just words.

– Noticing points of transitions of thought and how they connect to one another.

– Repetition - saying it over and over aloud. Glancing down only when necessary to quickly absorb the next phrase.

• TROUBLE SPOTS

When you come to a spot where you keep 'messing up' – work that section before you go on.

Thoughts & words before – – – – Trouble spot – – – – Thoughts & words after

(Refer to page 40 memorization)

Repeat that section until it flows without hesitation.

Note: *It's always good to review the copy closely in case you have changed some words that you thought you knew.*

• PICKING UP CUES

If there are other people in the spot with dialogue, it is not necessary to memorize their lines, (unless you are to switch roles) but it is necessary to become familiar enough with their dialogue so that you can react properly and come in with your lines on time. Pick Up Your Cues.

This is an important factor in commercial acting since time is such a strong factor. Even though it's an audition and not the actual filming of the spot, picking up your cues only benefits your performance. The more you know the material the better able you are to keep the dialogue flowing as opposed to leaving holes and breaking the rhythm.

Some "not too bright actors" know what **they** are saying and maybe just the last word of the speech before theirs. As they work on the copy, their approach is:

"he says something..., she says something... then I say ' _ _ _ _ _'"

This is a bad idea because it means there's no *listening* going on. The reactions aren't true or believable and if the person gives you the wrong word cue, you're lost. So take <u>heed</u> and be familiar with all of the copy.

Note: *The number of performers vary according to the situation, but if you do have to audition with someone, pray that they know what they're doing and rehearse with them, if possible. Theoretically, it's not supposed to matter if you go in with a 'dud', it just makes your job harder.*

• IT'S YOUR TURN

They call your name or your group to come in *so gather your picture, size sheet, copy and your nerves.*

If you get that familiar adrenalin rush, just take a couple of deep breaths from your center of energy (fully inhaling and exhaling) which will calm you down and help you to focus.

No matter how many people are in the room, your focus goes to the person giving you directions.

• LISTEN AND FOLLOW DIRECTIONS

Commercial acting can be very technical, involving very specific actions and hitting very specific marks. Your technical abilities are just as important as your artistic abilities. If you have any intentions of getting the job you're auditioning for, it is imperative that you listen and follow directions. If you think that what you're being asked to do is a little strange or weird, then so be it.... Quite often commercials call for the unusual. You can certainly ask for clarification or explanation if there is any, although sometimes the only reason for a certain direction is because that's the way they want it. Of course it is always your prerogative to choose not to do something that you don't feel is right, or you feel you can't handle, with the understanding that you just won't do this job. If you do intend to do the job, then you should listen, follow, and carry out the directions to the best of your ability, making them work in the scene. Pay special attention to directions concerning handling the product, making sure the action is done at the right time, on the right line, and in the right way.

• MAKE MENTAL NOTES

...of any marks you're supposed to hit, and incorporate the action with the line or thought so that it becomes a part of your performance and not just one more direction you need to remember.

• CHANGES

The CD may instruct you to use a different emotion or attitude on a certain line. They may even change the dialogue.

Absorb the direction immediately and work it into your performance, letting go of any previous instructions given you, or ideas you may have had.

Always be open, flexible, and ready for change. The work you have done on your cold readings, changing attitudes and emotions, and reading your material in different ways should help prepare you to be flexible.

• OTHER'S DIRECTIONS

Listen also to directions being given to other actors so you know what's going on, react properly, pick up your cues, and change roles if directed.

• IMPROVISE

If you're given a direction to create some dialogue or improvise until you hear a certain cue or before you make a certain move, be careful not to get so caught up in your creativity that you:

1. Talk so long and so loudly you overshadow the real dialogue.

2. Talk so much that you miss your cue.

3. Drag the dialogue or improv on so long that you lose track of the main objective or action you are to perform.

• BEWARE OF BEING DEFENSIVE

... because you've rehearsed something a certain way or were previously directed differently and they now want to change it.

Make the adjustment and go on. It is their prerogative to make changes and it is the nature of the business.

• QUESTIONS

If you have any questions about your performance or a direction, don't be afraid to ask. Even if you are not sure of something after you go through it once (rehearsal or taping) ask for clarification so you do better the next time.

• REHEARSAL

Most of the time you'll get a rehearsal, but if you don't, or you feel you need another one, ask for it. It may or may not be given but you can try.

• FEEL THE ROOM

Check out the mood of the audition room. If it is very relaxed and playful, it may be okay and even to your benefit to socialize and joke around a little bit.

– BUT –

Keep a check on it, don't miss anything important, and don't force it. If there is a lot of fooling around and talking going on in the midst of directions being given, make sure you focus on what you're being told to do and that you're clear on it before you perform. It's alright to have fun, but keep in mind the reason you're there.

On the other hand, the atmosphere may be serious or even solemn after a long day of auditioning. Don't take on the responsibility of cheering everybody up, just go in, be pleasant, and do your job.

• COPY vs. CUE CARDS

In the audition room the copy is usually written on a cue card and they ask you to use that instead of the paper you were given. With a larger print that can be easily seen from a distance, the copy is handprinted on cards about 2-1/2' x 1-1/2'. The cards are usually set across the room from the actor and close to the camera. The words may be placed or spaced differently on the card, so if you're used to referring to your paper in a certain way, you have got to readjust your vision and quickly get used to seeing words in a different place.

When there is more than one person with lines, they are usually written in different colors, so determine what color your lines are and where they are on the card so that your eye can go to them easily.

So while you're being given directions or other things are going on, look at the cue card, get familiar with it and give yourself as much rehearsal as you can on your own.

• THE CAMERA IS A 'PERSON'

And that person is standing right in front of you and not way across the room (where the camera actually may be). So, if you are directed to play to camera, you don't have to reach out to it, poke your head forward, or talk any louder than normal. You just stand back and be there, focusing on the camera eye as if you were looking into a person's eyes, talking to a friend. This will help you to internalize what you are doing as opposed to acting it out. (Note: Anything can change at the request of a director.)

• THE SLATE

The first thing the casting director puts on tape of you is your slate. This is usually done by asking you to stand on a mark indicated by an "X" or a line of tape on the floor like this " _____ " or this "T". At this point, you **wait for the action cue** from the director, then on action you look directly into camera and give your name. It is important to wait for the action cue, because the person operating the camera has to first focus on you and then roll tape before you begin. Sometimes, besides your name, you're also asked to give your agent and for children, your age. This is your first contact with the live camera and the first picture they see of you when viewing the tape. We all know how important that first impression is, and what you should want to impress on those viewing the tape is that you are:

1. confident

2. relaxed

3. pleasant to be around

4. and the right person for the job.

Director Mark Bernolt, stated that the slate tells him a lot about the person outside of the character in the commercial. So indeed, we want our slate to tell the right story. Beware of appearing cocky or disinterested. Like I said, you want to give a feeling of confidence, but you also want to give the impression that you're easy to work with. It does not have to be a performance within itself but only an introduction and an opportunity for you to get in touch with yourself and your viewing audience. Remember the voice warmup you did before you arrived, well now is the time to make contact with the strength in your diaphragm, using that center of your energy to control any nervousness and to project your voice in a natural confident manner. As you pull up in your center, take a nice easy cleansing breath and you're ready. Being very natural and personable, making contact with the camera as if it were a person, do your slate: "Hi" or "Hello, I'm (Your name) with (Your agency)". Only give the agency if it is asked for, and "Hi" or "Hello" is optional, you can just say your name.

Sometimes you can have a little fun with the slate and make it a little brighter or in some way related to the type of part you're playing if it is a special character. For instance, if the part calls for an accent, you can do your slate with an accent. If the part calls for a lot of comedy, you can do a more animated slate; a very professional business person, a sophisticated slate. This can help get you in the mood for what you're about to do. In any case, keep it **simple**, **honest**, and **easy**.

• PROFILE

Following the slate, you are sometimes asked to give your profiles which involve you turning to the left and then right (or vice versa) and giving your side view to the camera. This is a very simple thing to do but make a mental note that while you're freshening up, to be sure your back half is in order, hair, collar, etc. Sometimes I have a little fun with the profiles according to the mood in the room and of the commercial. Since my name has three parts, Vernée Watson Johnson, when I turn to one side I say "This is Watson", the other side, "This is Johnson", to the front, "And this is Vernée". This is a little silly thing that helps relax me and it's done within the context of something I have to do anyway, so it doesn't waste time.

Along with the profile, they may also do a full length shot so be aware of your posture, neatness, and stance. Ladies, if you're going for the business type, it is better to have heels in case of a full length. They give a better overall picture with a business suit than flats do. Guys who wear tennis shoes or just unpolished shoes with suits thinking they'll never show on camera, in a full length, they will be noticed, so take heed and be prepared.

• PLAYING TO CAMERA

When viewing the audition tapes and deciding who will book the commercial, the director and client want to see as much of your face as possible. Whether you are directed to play directly to camera or to someone or something off camera, it is important that they see your face, your eyes, and your expressions so they can get a real sense of who you are.

When playing directly to camera, the movement of your eyes is very visible. They should be focusing directly into the lens more than looking at the cue card. So if you have to refer to the cue card use the cold reading techniques we practiced in Chapter One.

Glance at the card, absorbing a complete thought and phrase at a time, then back to camera.

Playing thought by thought instead of word by word will help your pauses to seem more natural, and give you a better sense of where the line is going so you can make the proper inflections and give the proper meaning.

• CHEATING TO CAMERA

When you're playing to someone else and not directly to camera make sure your face can be seen by the camera and you are not upstaging yourself by showing the back of your head or just a little of your face. Your eyes can be on the person you're speaking to but your face is turned more toward the camera. This is called cheating to camera. Also try to keep your body angled toward the camera instead of a profile or back unless you're directed otherwise.

THE PERFORMANCE

• AUDITIONS ARE PERFORMANCES

It's time to really focus and not worry about what you look like, what they think of you, or whether or not you're going to get this job that you need so badly. It's time to do the job of auditioning. If you really focus in on what you're doing, you'll have plenty to keep your mind occupied without clouding it with doubt or worry and before you know it, the audition is over and you will have done a good job, had a great experience, and had another opportunity to book a commercial. Even if you mess up in a few, you learn from the experience and know that the more you do, the better you'll get.

WHAT ELEMENTS MAKE UP A GOOD COMMERCIAL PERFORMANCE?

We've already talked about the first element and that is:

• CONFIDENCE

Your audience (this is what we'll call the CD, Director, and Clients) feels confident if you feel confident. This confidence comes from being familiar with the material, feeling good about yourself as an actor, and being secure with the choices you have made. If you're lacking in any of these areas, you can still be confident that this will be a good experience for you and you will try your best.

• CONCENTRATION

I like to refer to this as **Focusing**: Keeping your mind centered on only the thoughts your character is thinking. Commercial acting, being a very technical art, requires that you also remain focused on your dialogue and actions which leaves no room for being concerned about any other extraneous matters that you may not have any control over. Focus.

• **ARTICULATION**

(Unless you're doing a dialect or an accent, you should use the correct pronunciation of all the words.) If you've done your work, this should come very easily during the performance. Remember to keep the lips and tongue relaxed and flexible so they can work properly and use the diaphragm. If you have a lot of copy, be aware not to gasp for air between phrases. Lift up, let the air drop in, filling up through a loose mouth and this can happen very quickly without making noise. Also, with a lot of copy, try not to sound rushed. Keep it going at a good pace, but leave room for expression. They'll let you know if they need it faster. In articulating, you don't have to over pronounce your words as you did for some of your exercises, but use correct pronunciation in a natural way as if this is the way you talk all the time. You should project, but not as though you were on stage, unless directed differently. Remember, there's a mic overhead to pick up your voice and you want to speak at a natural level, being careful not to swallow the sounds and words in the effort. So let us hear you and give us the words.

• **CREATIVE EXPRESSION**

This pertains to giving different levels and colors to your performance; not making all the obvious and ordinary choices, but making intelligent, interesting choices; -- giving different levels to your intensity, attitudes and inflections, painting a picture and giving meaning to words that could easily sound corny or stilted, giving variety in your voice levels, using the diaphragm so your voice won't crack or go way up in your head. Have fun with it!

• **PERSONALIZATION**

No matter what character you're playing, you consciously or unconsciously bring part of yourself into it. Never try to completely cut yourself off from your character. In most cases, unless otherwise directed, it is best to add as much of yourself as possible.

• SPONTANEITY

This element really blends in with personalization and creative expression. Make the words sound like your own, as if this is something you came up with just this moment, unrehearsed. Many commercials are leaning toward a very real feel, so personalization is very important. Let your personality come through as you use creative expression. Your actions, though they may be specifically directed, should look like part of your natural movement or a natural reaction. Being confident and being able to let go and just kick into doing the performance helps in adding spontaneity. Things may happen in an audition that you had no idea you would do, and that work well!!

• SPECIALIZATION

Make the information you're giving very special and desirable and make your audience want to listen. You have something to tell them that they need to know about. You've found this great product that will solve their problem. I'm not talking about hard sell – because that's pretty taboo for the most part – but about having a belief in what you're saying with a quiet excitement and energy behind it. If your copy has a list of descriptive words or various items, make each one **special** and **important**. Remember to work internally and have it come from a real feeling or belief and not just some external, contrived emotion. Believe what you're saying and make it special.

• TRANSITION

Going from one thought to another – – a transition is the way in which one thought develops or evolves from another. Transition in thought also creates transition in attitude or emotion. If you have done your work, you know where the transitions are, but if you do loose your place and have to refer to the copy or cue card, make sure you get the complete picture and know when the transition is supposed to come. This will help make your delivery smooth and you won't have to shift gears in the middle of a phrase or go back and say it over. **Know where the changes are.**

• CONTINUITY

With all the transitions, personalizations and creativity, **the copy still must flow and make sense**. After all is said and done, the audience must get a clear picture of what you are saying. **Knowing the overall thought behind the commercial is the main ingredient in continuity**. It also helps your performance have a strong ending because you know where you're going. Everything in the spot is done or said for a reason and everything is somehow connected. Finding and using that connecting line will help you keep your continuity. **Let it flow and make sense.**

• INTERNALIZING

All your thoughts, emotions, and expressions should come from within. Acting is being and is not an external display of emotion. The only way for you to act from within is to quiet down and truly believe and feel what you're doing. This prevents a lot of overacting and pushing which frequently occurs in auditions. Because the current trends are towards more realism, internalizing is a most important factor of your performance and a key to being real and natural. It just involves knowing what your thoughts are, quieting down and thinking them, and not feeling that you have to perform or demonstrate like 'show and tell'. If you're really thinking and feeling, then it will come.

• USING NERVOUS TENSION

The majority of performers, whether secure or insecure, will get an adrenalin rush before a performance. You can label it what you want and you can use it positively or negatively. Most of us are familiar with the negative use, allowing fear to take over or letting insecurity get in our way. *Use it in a positive sense as an extra bit of energy to get those creative juices flowing to make you brighter and more interesting.* Don't sink down into it but pull up out of it and use it to your benefit. We've all heard of people being able to lift cars in a crisis. Well an audition can be a little crisis which is why you're given the extra adrenalin. Use it Positively.

• RECALL

This is also very important, especially while shooting, and is a mark of a true professional. That is to be aware of how you're playing something and what you're doing so that you will be able to repeat that performance or alter it as directed. When Mark and I discussed this he said that, as a director, in working with a non-professional, you have to move them in very specific ways and work very hard to get the desired results. If you are a professional, you should be flexible and not only able to duplicate your performance but also be able to recall what you've done and make the fine adjustments that may be required.

• TIME

There is a definite time element involved in auditioning, although it's not that critical. All your work on the copy and performance has to be done quickly and the more you do it the better you'll become. You don't have to worry about specific time until you actually shoot the commercial, but you should be aware to keep the pace moving.

We've gone through quite a few elements of performance, but let's understand that not all of them will be used all the time. However, the more knowledge you have, the more choices you will have available to you.

• MAKING MISTAKES

In any situation, if you mess up or flub a word, just correct it in a calm manner and continue on as if you just made a natural mistake. Don't stop everything and make a big deal out of it, call yourself 'a dope' or use the "S" word. It doesn't need that kind of attention. The better you handle it, the better they will handle it. Remember, they react from your actions, so if you give it very little attention, correct it and move on, they won't view it as a major flaw in your performance.

If you do happen to stop because you messed up, then it is okay to ask to start again. Sometimes the CD may even suggest it. But, unless you're actually filming the spot, it's quite often not necessary to do it over and any flub can be viewed as part of natural conversation. Another point is to be very careful not to criticize yourself mentally or verbally immediately after you've finished your performance or after they say "cut". Even if you just *think* something negative about your performance, it will show on your face and may be put on tape at the end of your audition and be the last impression they get of you. It looks bad and doesn't help anything, so keep those criticisms in your pocket and save them until you're out and away from there, then calmly critique your work, good or bad, and learn from it.

• AFTER THE AUDITION

After the audition, your job is done so release it and go on. I found that, since I don't wear make-up normally, if after the audition, I wash my face and change back into my normal comfortable stuff, it helps me to release any stress concerning the audition and encourages me to move on to the next thing.

PART 2

PRACTICE WORK ON COMMERCIAL COPY

In Chapter One I suggested you work on practice copy from magazine ads, TV, etc. Now let's get more practical experiences with copy that is closer to what you will be handed at an audition.

I've made up some commercials that follow the general trend. Let's review them and see, first hand, how the copy breakdown works and when and where the elements fit in.

As I mentioned before, the time you have to work on copy at an actual audition is limited, so the more practice you get in breaking down copy and working the elements, the quicker you will be able to dissect the material and get to performance level at an audition.

PRACTICE SPOT #1

This copy can be used by a girl or guy. Pick out your own props that would be approximately the same size and shape of a liquid household cleanser. The character is a mom or dad. It's a :30 (second) spot, but you may only have :25 (seconds) for dialogue. The call on the spot would probably be "nice casual, very real, lots of dialogue".

ALL-IN-ONE

Life is serious enough without having to make major decisions on household cleansers.

There are so many different brands, with such complicated ingredients, that you'd almost have to be a chemist to figure them out.

Thank goodness for All-In-One.

All the things I need in one convenient container. It's biodegradable and non-toxic, so it

won't hurt the environment or your mischievous
children.
   All-In-One.
It's all I need and one less problem to deal with.

Let's read it out loud to see if we have any problems with enunciation. The first sentence doesn't contain any tongue twisters but make sure, here and throughout, that you are articulating the full words and not slurring over them or leaving off the end sounds, i.e., without, having, household, cleansers.

In the second sentence, the *'th'* in *'with'* needs to be clear and flow right into the *'s'* in *'such'*. *'Complicated ingredients'* has quite a few syllables that need work, and be sure to get all the *'t'* s' in *'that'*, *'almost'*, *'chemist'*, *'to'* and *'out'*. The next sentence contains the product name *'All-In-One'*, so pronounce it as a title of the product and not just a group of words. *'Convenient'* may give some people trouble because of the 'nient' and then going right back into the *'c'* and *'t'* sounds in *'container'*. Say them together over and over until they flow. Remember to practice using the whole sentence so that it'll all work together. The same goes for the stumblers in the next sentence; *'biodegradable'*, *'non-toxic'*, *'environment'*, and *'mischievous children'*. Mischievous should be pronounced with emphasis on the first syllable. In the last sentences, again the product is important and be careful of the *'th'* in *the things* –and the *'to'* not *'ta'*– and the *'th'* in *'with'* in *'to deal with'*. Work out all the kinks until you can say it clearly, smoothly and naturally.

Now let's do a **Copy Breakdown** together. You may work it differently, but let's get the general idea.

1. Overall thought and point being made. All-In-One helps to make your life simple. With all the stress we have, All-In-One is a good solution.

2. What they want the consumer to know and feel, descriptive words or

phrases. That All-In-One is conveniently packaged and it won't hurt the environment or your children. --words and phrases: serious, major, complicated, convenient, biodegradable, non-toxic, mischievous, All-In-One, all I need, one less problem.

3. Transitions.

> You'd almost... them out.   (transition) Thank goodness...
> You go from explaining a problem you're having.
> – to –
> Being thankful for finding a solution.
> ...mischievous children.   (transition)   All-In-One.
> You go from protecting your curious children
> – to –
> Admiration for product.

4. Points of comparison; complexity vs. simple,   safe vs. unsafe

5. Benefits: better because it's simple & safe.

6. Points of conflict or objections: Not in this spot.

Answering these questions and noting these points about the copy should help you a great deal in your performance.

To memorize, let's go through the copy several times, looking away from the paper and focusing on a spot whenever possible as if talking to a friend. Don't just say lines but think the thoughts behind the lines and how they connect or move from one to another.

Memorize a phrase or complete thought at a time instead of trying to memorize words.

For instance;

<u>Life is serious enough</u>   <u>without having to make major decisions</u> <u>on household cleansers</u>.

<u>There are so many different brands</u>   <u>with such complicated</u>

<u>ingredients,</u>

<u>that you'd almost have to be a chemist to figure them out.</u>

<u>Thank goodness for All-In-One.</u>

<u>All the things I need</u>   <u>in one convenient container.</u>

<u>It's biodegradable and non toxic,</u>   <u>so it won't hurt the environment</u>

<u>or your mischievous children.</u>

<u>All-In-One.</u>   <u>It's all I need</u>   <u>and one less problem to deal with.</u>

If there are any spots where you can't figure out what's next, work on it as we did on page 71 "Trouble Spots".

•DIRECTIONS

Let's do this one in two different ways with two different sets of directions.

1. Play it all to camera as if you're telling it to a friend.

    − There's no action on the first two lines except to relate directly to camera.

    − On the lines "Thank goodness for All-In-One", <u>pick up the product</u> with the right hand on the word "thank".

    − Hold the product about shoulder height, close to your face, and showing the label. Keep it there in a relaxed way during the next line, "all the things .... container."

    − Pat the side of the container with the left hand on "in one convenient",

    − Point to the label, referring to the words "biodegradable" and "non toxic" as you say them.

    − Put the container down during, "so it won't hurt the environment...

    − Hear children playing offstage, react, deliver, "or your mischievous children"

- You pick it back up on "All-In-One", looking at it on that line.

- Then turn to camera and deliver the last line, as you put the product down.

- Don't let your eyes go down with the product, but stay focused into camera, feeling good about finding the product.

2. Playing to Camera With Moves:

- From upstage right, take 4 steps toward camera as if you're walking down a supermarket aisle with your children coming to the cleanser section. The shelves are up on your right but close to camera left. The cart you're pushing is down to your left (camera right) but angled close to camera.

- Start speaking on the third step and stop on your mark on the fourth.

- The first sentence is played to camera, reacting off of some disturbance from your kids.

- Look at shelves on "There are so many .... ingredients",

- Back to camera on "You'd almost have to be ... them out."

- Reach for the product on the shelf with your right hand on "Thank goodness"

- Pick it up on "for".

- Bring it close to your face on "All-In-One".

- Look at the product on "All the things I need...".

- Place it in the shopping cart on "... in one convenient container".

- Play the next sentence to camera "It's biodegradable ... mischievous children", reacting off the kids at the end of it.

Time Lapse
[In 2 beats (seconds) for our purposes]

- A new scene. We see you talking through a window in front of you holding the product in your right hand with a cloth in the left.
- Say "All-In-One" to camera
- Quickly spritz the window and wipe then,
- Say to camera through the clean spot "All the things I need..."
- Quickly discover a spot you've missed, spritz and wipe as you say to camera "... and one less problem to deal with."

As you can see, the directions are very specific in both versions. Make your moves naturally and on time. Practice until the moves work well with the dialogue.

You may use a physical product or practice pantomine. In pantomine, make the product, the space in the market, the shelves and the shopping cart, real for yourself.

Don't ever cover your face with the product and don't cover the label on the product with your fingers.

THE ELEMENTS

• **CONFIDENCE**

Your confidence will come from knowing the words and the moves.

• **CONCENTRATION**

Focus on what you're doing. Your actions, words and belief in the product.

• **CREATIVE EXPRESSION and PERSONALIZATION**

Play all the different colors and levels. From the serious tone of the opening, to a little humor in "having to make major decisions on household cleansers."

Next, you go from making a statement about a complex situation to being thankful and relieved about finding a solution.

Then you're feeling good about the benefits of the product and adding your own personal touch on "mischievous children", like we all know what you mean. Say the product name with more conviction the second time. On the last line you can use confidence and reassurance, then even a little more humor and personality on "one less problem to deal with."

• SPONTANEITY

Start the spot like you just thought of something serious and you're relieved that this is going to be an easy decision. The words come as you go.

• ARTICULATION

This is the work you did on your words and troublespots.

• SPECIALIZATION

By being confident in the product and believing in what you're saying, you are making your information very special and desirable.

• TRANSITIONS

We covered those in the breakdown. (Pg. 87)

• CONTINUITY

Connecting your thoughts by stating a problem, finding a solution, giving the benefits, then showing your confidence and gratitude. Make these thoughts and the transitions of thought smooth to help your delivery have a nice natural flow.

• INTERNALIZING

Now take your performance with all it's colors and internalize it, bring it from within, being real and natural. Any nervous tension you feel, you control it with your center of energy.

• RECALL

Work on your recall. Do your performance the same several times, then alter your delivery slightly in different areas. Make your performance broader and more expressive then tone it down. Change your readings on various lines, putting a different thought or attitude behind it, then use recall to practice duplicating it.

ie. "Your mischievous children"
   - those cute little devils (with a smile)
   - those overactive children (with concern)

OR

The opening line
"Life can be .... on household cleansers"
   - very emphatic, like you really don't need more problems
   - or lighter, like we all know how bad it can get, let's not waste stress on household cleansers. (with a little humor)

Remember, on each variation, repeat it to make sure you remember what you did.

• TIME

Realize that since you're studying, you're taking quite a bit of time to analyze the copy and work on your performance. This practice will help you get the most out of the copy and the more you do it the less time it will take. We have already discussed that time is very limited in auditioning, so all of this work must sometimes be done in 5 minutes or less.

Even though this is a :30 spot, your dialogue may be only 23-25 seconds. Get yourself a cheap stopwatch and practice shaving and adding seconds. The more you familiarize yourself with the process, the easier it gets.

The same holds true for all the elements until they become a natural part of your performance.

PRACTICE SPOT #2
Allergy Release

Here's another spot where you have to add some other elements to your performance.

My hay fever...
My nose never stops running
My eyes are itchy and watery (sneeze)
You name it, I've got it.
(time lapse after use of product)
... Finally some relief

• COPY BREAKDOWN

1. Overall thought – the uncomfortable annoying symptoms of hay fever can be relieved by this product. (They're using the interview method and visualization of the symptoms, followed by relief).

2. What they want us to know – symptoms of hay fever can be relieved by this product.

3. Transitions – the big transition comes between "you name it I've got it –– – finally some relief". (physical and mental transition –– figure it out)

4. No obvious points of comparision except one can assume that you have tried other brands without getting any relief and this brand is finally different and better.

5. Benefits – relief from running nose, itchy watery eyes, stuffy head, sneezing.

6. Conflicts or objections: None.

In these spots, there are some physical elements being played as well as emotional. You need the emotional elements to make it believable; focusing and internalizing your thoughts and feelings, so that it doesn't come out phoney.

• DIRECTIONS AND USE OF ELEMENTS

I'm combining the two because your performance elements should come into play as you go along.

- First of all you should have all the symptoms: stuffy head, irritated eyes, nasal voice, and you could sneeze at any moment. In order to be believable, unless you're suffering from them as we speak, you'll have to use recall. Don't overdo it and don't put on for an affect. Internalize and Personalize. Really feel and be uncomfortable.

- Because of your stuffy head your voice has a nasal tone but we should still understand the words...

- The first line is said as if someone just asked you, "Do you have hay fever? Tell us about it." So, you're listening at the open and then responding.

- As you describe the symptoms, you're feeling all of them, all the time, not just becoming aware of them as you go. You're already aware of them and just deciding which one you'll tell us about first.

- After "My eyes are itchy and watery", give a real unaffected <u>sneeze</u>, not too big. Stay away from the obvious build-up of the sneeze during the "...itchy watery", line. Just let it happen spontaneously even though you naturally try to suppress it.

- Stay in frame. The camera would be in a tight head shot, so when you sneeze don't drop your head out of frame.

– Right after the sneeze (which should be one or two seconds at the most) go right into, "You name it, I've got it", as if the sneeze spoke for itself as one of your many symptoms.

– Time lapse and a big transition.*

Collect yourself. You have taken the product, you can breathe easier and your eyes have stopped burning.

Make your adjustment internally and after two beats, give a small sigh, take a look at the product that's in your hand, then feeling better and grateful, say to camera "...Finally, some relief."

The transition – For audition purposes the <u>time lapse</u> must be done quickly and we must really sense that you feel better. This is an important transition and can be directed different ways, but for now make it definite but small. Too big of a change may make it look like you've never been sick. Just think in terms of finally being able to breathe, talk, and see clearly.

– Say this is a :15 spot. Your total dialogue should take between :10 and :12. Use your stopwatch to practice these different times.

• ALTERNATE DIRECTIONS

Here are some different ways to play, " You name it, I've got it".
– Like you're just miserable and see no help in sight.
– As if you're saying, "...and you think you have problems."

Here are some different ways to play "Finally, some relief". Try them for variation and then use recall to repeat them.
– A little surprise that your head is clear.
– Thank goodness for this product.
– You never thought it would happen.
– Create some of your own

PRACTICE SPOT #3

Flu Release

Hay fever is just one of the things you may have to act out. Another could be a chest cold, or a cold with the flu, that means having chills, an aching body, and a bad cough. Try this one in the same tone as #2. Do your own breakdown and use the elements.

... My flu ...
I've got chills
My body aches all over
My head is killing me and everytime I try to rest... (bad cough)
... I've got it bad.
(time lapse --- look at product, then to camera)
..... Finally some relief.

We have all felt these symptoms at some time or another, but the degree to which you are able to recall them and use them in your performance will determine the sincerity of your audition.

Make up a commercial on muscle ache, menstrual pain, or back pain. See how many aches and pains you can come up with, recall, and make real for yourself. The good part is that you can let go of them at will.

PRACTICE SPOT #4

Here's another commercial with a different flavor where you're feeling terrific! It could be done by two people or you can do it alone. It should be done with a lot of energy and personality and gives good practice in articulation.

Take Five Super Snacks

When I take a break and need a little lift
I grab hold to a Take Five Super Snack.
These great little snacks give me the punch
I need to go back to work with a fresh start.
And now New Take Five Super Snacks Lite
are low in calories, so they give me the

(Continued next page)

energy I need and leave the fat behind.
Take Five Super Snacks and
New Take Five Super Snacks Lite.
Great taste in a powerful little pack.

Do your own breakdown, but I'll give you some tips and directions.

—   I'm sure you noticed that the product title is quite long: "Take Five Super Snacks" and "New Take Five Super Snacks Lite." They should be said as one name so be careful to keep the words together and let them flow so they sound like one unit. Your lips and tongue really have to be working in order to articulate properly.

—   These characters are very active people with busy schedules so the energy level is very high. Pay special attention to the action words and phrases such as: *...I grab hold... the punch I need... the energy I need... a powerful little pack...* These phrases have force behind them so make sure you use them in such a way that we feel that energy. Even in the title, "Take Five Super Snacks" implies that it's not just ordinary, but something special and powerful.

• **DIRECTIONS**   *(We'll do several different characters)*

1. School teacher – Scene: The bell has just rung to dismiss a class of very active children.

   —   Ad lib an opening line like:

   "That's it, I'll see you all tomorrow."

   –OR–

   "Remember your assignments and no running in the halls."

–OR–

Make up your own

The ad lib is done standing at the blackboard, just finishing a lesson, talking to the students. Make it short, but let the audience feel that you've worked hard and you're ready for a break.

- Then take a seat at your desk, pull the snack out from your desk drawer and deliver the lines to camera.

- By the time you get to the product title, you should have opened the package.

- Take a bite after saying the product name.

- As if you have received instant energy, deliver the next line. *"These great..."*

- After the phrase "*...the punch I need...*" the bell will ring and another group of children will start to enter the classroom.

- As you stand preparing for the next class, deliver the rest of the line "*to go back... start*".

- Time lapse -- change of character or an extension of the first character.
  You're at home, taking a quick break from exercising. You have been exercising and perspiring but at the moment we see you, you're wiping your face with a towel, using your left hand, and taking a bite of a Super Snack with the other. Do this action quickly and let us know it tastes good and gives you a lift.

- Then deliver the line..." And now New Take... are low in calories", showing the product to camera.

- Put it down after the word "calories".

- Go back to your exercise routine on "... so they give me the energy I need and leave the fat behind." On the last part of the phrase, motion behind you but keep it clean and fun.

– Another <u>time lapse</u> and actually the last 3 lines would probably be voice overs, but for audition purposes, we'll say them on camera. Hold both products, and as you say each name, hold that package up to camera so they both end up side by side. Then in the last line on the word "powerful", give them a little squeeze indicating their power.

Here are some tips:

– Work thru your performance elements as described on page 79 adding colors, making it believable, keeping it natural and real.

– Whenever you're holding the product, be careful not to cover the label and this goes for any commercial. In this particular one, even on the squeeze, do it with your finger tips.

– When you are directed to eat in a spot, get in the habit of taking smaller bites and acting like you're taking big juicy ones. It is to your benefit for several reasons. You won't fill up too quickly if you have to do a lot of takes. You won't consume a lot, if the food doesn't agree with you. You'll be able to speak more clearly in a shorter amount of time, because you can swallow it faster.

– Since you were not given a specific exercise to do, you should pick one that you do well, and show that it really takes some energy to do. Choose one that will enable you to play to camera not causing you to look away, and that doesn't require a lot of hand movement that will distract from your close ups.

Now do your own copy breakdown:

1. Overall thought – method of selling

2. What they want you to feel or know.

3. Transitions, Changes in thought, emotion, and time.

4. Points of comparison

5. Benefits.

6. Conflicts or objections.

Now try the same commercial using these variations in character.

1. Conducting a seminar	6. Athlete
2. Construction Worker	7. Housewife
3. Dance Teacher	8. Mom – Dad
4. Mail Person	9. Counter Person
5. Student	10. Create Your Own

PRACTICE SPOT #5

Here is another commercial. The type is upscale casual and it's played directly to camera. This one is done in another format that is sometimes used; the directions on the left side and the copy on the right.

Advertising Agency Name Client's Name: :30 second film or :30 TV Title: "A Dessert Lover's Dream"	Address: Job #: Revision # and Date: Product: Ultra Light Pudding Dessert Cups

Close up on person talking directly to camera, very conversational.	<u>Lady/Man</u>: If a dessert doesn't taste very good, why eat it. Then again, most desserts cost too much in calories.
Camera pulls back a little to reveal the person holding a dessert cup in one hand and a spoon in the other. Stirring the pudding.	However, New Ultra Light Pudding Dessert Cups are just as delicious as regular Pudding Dessert Cups but only 100 calories, and free of fat and cholesterol.
CU of product. *Vanilla and strawberry pudding.*	And they come in the same terrific flavors ... Vanilla .... strawberry ...
Taking a spoonful, eating and loving it.	... this one's chocolate.
Camera pulls back to reveal a slim trim figure	Um. It's a dessert lovers dream and doesn't cost extra on the arms or legs.
Voice over on product shot.	Annoc. VO: Ultra Light Pudding Dessert Cups -- A dessert lover's dream.

This format actually gives you more information as to what's happening in the commercial than those containing only the copy. Even though the phrases are broken up, the words and thoughts should still flow quickly because it's only a :30 spot. You do not say the announcers lines, but you must leave 4 to 5 seconds for them and product shots so your lines should be done in :24 or :25 at the most. Again, the product title is very long but should sound like one name, so work on your articulation. The directions given say that it should be conversational which means focusing, being very natural, and adding your own personality.

Do a Copy Breakdown:

1.   Overall Thought – Method of Selling.

2.   What do they want the consumer to feel or know about the product?

3.   Transitions.

4.   Points of comparison.

5.   Benefits.

6.   Conflicts or objections

Remember your elements of performance:

Confidence	Specialization
Concentration	Transition
Creative Expression	Continuity
Articulation	Internalizing
Personalization	Time
Spontaneity	

Use different levels of intensity and variations in attitude and see if you can duplicate them.

PRACTICE SPOT #6

Now let's move on to another type of commercial, using more than one person. Get two other people to work on it with you and exchange roles so that each person gets a chance to do all three parts at performance level. The product is non-descript, but the characters should be very well defined, each one having their own personality. This is a very tight :30 spot and it is done very up tempo. The lines come right on top of each other without overlapping. Aside from other things, it will be a good exercise in picking up cues.

THE CUSTOMER IS ALWAYS RIGHT

Customer comes in ready to fuss and complain about anything, and brings the damaged product to a very polite and patronizing salesperson, who is getting ready to pack up the good product for customer #2.

Customer #1:
Excuse me, I'd like to exchange this for another one. It has a dent in it.
Salesperson:
Of course, the customer's always right. I'll take care of it as soon as I finish here.

Paying for his/her superior product, customer #2 is feeling good about his or her decision.

Customer #2:
Okay, you say this is the best. I'll take your word for it.

Very Reassuring.

Salesperson:
That's right. It'll certainly get the job done.

Confused, and ready to catch the salesperson in a lie.

Customer #1:
Wait a minute, you said mine would get the job done.

Salesperson is being as honest and patronizing as usual. Giving them what they want.

Salesperson:
That's right. Yours isn't quite as sturdy as this one, but it costs less and you said you wanted a bargain. The customer's always right.

Very self-righteous.

Customer #2:
You get what you pay for.

Agreeable.

Salesperson:
That's right.

Pushing the other product aside, having decided to spend the extra money, indicates he/she wants the better brand stacked behind the salesperson.

Customer #1:
Well, I've changed my mind. I'll take one of those.

Giving new package to customer #1.

Salesperson:
Of course.

Customer #2 sticks his/her "two cents in".

Customer #2:
Good choice.

Getting ready to say his/her favorite line.

Salesperson:
Remember ...

Knowing the story, they both finish it off.

Customer #1 & #2:
The customer's always right.

Same bright agreeable self as he/she finishes up with both customers.

Salesperson:
That's right!

To work on this spot, as I stated, it would help if you had two other people. Although in an audition, the casting person may read the other two peoples' lines and you just read your own. So if you have one other person, they can do just that, and you play directly to camera, putting the third imaginary person off to camera right or left.

In a spot like this, it would really help to be familiar with all the lines and work through it until you get the timing and rhythm down. Picking up your cues is most important, which means listening and knowing your lines.

Work on each one of the characters, one at a time of course, and make each one separate, with personalities based on the information you've been given in the directions. Aside from picking up your cues and listening to the other actors, you also have business or specific action to do.

•DIRECTIONS

They are written in the copy on the left side.

The copy breakdown will be different for each character. We'll do customer #1 together and the others, you should do on your own. Some of the answers will be the same since they deal with the overall spot.

•BREAKDOWN FOR CUSTOMER #1

1. Overall thought - in one sentence "You get what you pay for": Even though this is customer #2's line, it is still the overall thought of the spot.

   Method of selling – a comparison of the quality of a cheaper product to a better brand.

2. What they want the consumer to feel or know:

   Even though a cheaper brand may get the job done, the product probably won't last because it's not as durable.

3. Transitions:

    The first transition of thought begins while hearing customer #2 say that he/ she has the best product, then the salesperson's line "That's right... the job done". The thought goes from having doubts and questioning the salesperson's honesty, to deciding to spend the extra money for the better product.

    "Well I've changed my mind... the other brand".

    Then the last transition or change comes when you finish the salesperson's line "the customer's always right". You're admitting that you got what you asked for, but you don't feel bad about it because the salesperson was just doing his/her job.

4. Points of comparison:

    Price and durability. Looking for a bargain as opposed to spending a little more and getting a better product.

5. Benefits: This product not only gets the job done well, but lasts, and is strong.

6. Objections or conflicts: The salesperson told you that yours would do the job, now he's changing the story. The salesperson also says if you buy cheaply, don't expect the best.

These answers can be altered or changed to your own words, but the basics are there. Now do your breakdown for the other characters*. Remember some of the answers will be the same.

*uyop   (use your own paper)

•ELEMENTS

The elements are also very important in this spot because each character should be very different and specific. We've already discussed the element of time, so you know the importance of picking up those cues. Time it and see if you do it all in :30 seconds, with feeling.

PRACTICE SPOT #7

Now let's do one with a more serious professional tone. This takes place in a business meeting with four characters, each one with his or her own personality and function within the organization.

It is written very simply with the parts numbered.

"BEING PREPARED"

#1 Do we have the updated reports on our overseas holdings?

#2 I had the numbers on the Japan deal, but I didn't know they'd be on this morning's agenda.

#3 If you'd take a look at the reports in front of you, you'll find not only all the figures, but a graph of the current market trends.

#4 I was told we should cancel our foreign interests, based on long term analysis.

#3 I think we're all just a little anxious because of our recent expansion, but if you'd just take a look...

#1 Well I have been looking, and I think it's all laid out right here...

#4 (surprised) In color?

#2 This is quite impressive. Is this a result of our new system?

#3 That's right. Another good investment.

#1 Well I think we should just examine these to see where we stand.

ANNCR: Having all the information and being prepared is important in today's business world. So do it with ITM. A good investment.

• **DIRECTIONS**

– Each role can be played by either male or female, so practice and work on all four characters. For an actual audition, you would probably read with three other people and be asked to change roles.

– As in Practice Spot #6, the cues should be picked right up and it should flow quickly with the energy of an important business conference.

– If you get others to work with you, set up a conference table with a few props including pencils, folders (which contain the reports), pitcher of water and glasses.

– Create natural business for yourself during the spot, but make sure it doesn't get in the way of the dialogue.

– For practice purposes, I'll give you some character tips. You should work on them and really try to develop full characters so you can call upon them for actual auditions.

PERSON #1:   The one who holds a higher position than the others, and calls the shots. Very fair.

PERSON #2:   Never quite prepared, but always has something to say.

PERSON #3:   Conscientious, hard-working, proud of his or her work but knows the importance of working together.

PERSON #4:   A pessimist, jealous of others' hard work, but would prefer to talk than do. Listens to gossip.

You may notice that it's like a little play, and just as in a play the scene should have life. Work on it, doing a copy breakdown and using the elements until you get all four characters to performance level, each one being distinctively different. A good idea in this and the other commercials would be to make up your own cue cards (page 75) and put them next to camera or your camera mark. Make each character's dialogue a different color and practice using the cue card without being obvious. If you know one role too well, then change to another that you're unfamiliar with, so that you need to refer to the cue card at times.

COMMERCIALS WITH LITTLE OR NO DIALOGUE

Not all commercials have a lot of dialogue. Quite a number have very little dialogue or just one line. Some have only reactions, where you play your thoughts with no words /or mos (mit out sound) where you may be improvising dialogue, but it is not heard. In these types, you must really be able to relate emotions, make statements and transitions in thought, facial expression, and body language without the use of dialogue.

ONE LINERS

Let's work on some one-liners. These should be done directly to camera and at different levels of intensity. You can create what you're talking about, react to it and make it real and natural. Even though there may only be one line, the performance elements still apply. You should be very focused and the line should come from within. Don't let them be just external, unfelt outbursts, but internalize them and let them come from a real place so that they are believable, even the very strong reactions. I'll give you a variety, but you can always create your own or do variations on the ones I've given.

- It's great
- It's terrific
- I love it
- You don't say
- No problem
- No way
- I'm not sure
- No, I can't
- Yes, I can
- Not this one
- Tastes great
- It's delicious
- Uummm
- I won, I won!

- I see
- Is that so
- I don't believe it
- Not me
- Just for you
- Take it or leave it
- This is all I need
- It's just what I wanted
- Never
- All the time
- It really works
- What a relief
- It hurts so bad

Do each one several times with various levels and thoughts behind them.

REACTIONS

Now let's do some **reaction shots without dialogue, using the line as just a thought or suggestion**. Some should be done looking away from camera, then turning to camera with the reaction. Others can be done straight to camera.

- This is great
- I like it
- It's just what I wanted
- I'm not so sure
- Which one will it be
- That's it
- Oh my God
- I'm not very impressed
- I don't think so

- I feel great,
- My head is killing me
- I'm so full
- Tell me more
- You're kidding
- I don't believe you
- I don't feel so good
- What a relief
- What happened

Remember to do them at different levels so that you can become more aware of making changes and adjustments in your performance.

NO COPY – IMPROVISATIONAL SPOTS

These commercials are usually done with the announcer's voice and/or music over them, so that you don't hear the dialogue of the people on the screen. During your actual audition, you are heard and put on tape, so you want it to be real. The best ways to make it real are:

- Listen to the directions given to you and the other actors.
- Decide your relationship to the person or people you're working with and relate honestly to them.
- Picture your space.
- Put the business in front of you, playing to camera (unless directed otherwise).
- Actually see what you're talking about.
- If specific actions and cues are given to you, perform them clearly, believably and in the time frame of the spot.
- Play the moment. If something comes up that doesn't go along with what you've set up or thought about, play along with it and work with what is happening at the moment. Don't make obvious objections, and stop the flow of the scene.

GIVE AND TAKE

Creative dialogue and improvisations work best when it's give and take. **You give some of your creativity, and then you listen and react to another's input.** Try to make your actions and dialogue specific and clear, following the directions given, completing your objective in the proper amount of time.

Actors tend to drag out improvisations such as this, especially if they are connecting and things are happening. The problem with this is, in the midst of all this creative dialogue, the specific directions are barely recognizable. So, no matter how much fun you're having, remember to get to the point.

IMPROVS

Here's a couple of examples to give you an idea of how to create specifics.

1. Set Up: You and one other person are shopping in a department store, looking through several items until you find the perfect piece.

• DIRECTIONS

Decide your relationship to the person you're working with and what the specific item is that you need and why. Visualize the department store, seeing the racks and counters, and place them toward camera so that your action can be seen. After looking through several items, all appealing, but not quite right, at the height of your improv, find the perfect peice and give it's benefits. You can even include that the item is on sale, or how it works so well with different things.

This can be done by a mom or dad, son or daughter. For now, we'll use the mom – son combination.

2. Set Up: It's morning, mother is seated at the breakfast table just having finished her cereal, reading the paper, feeling good. Son comes in and tells his mother he's in a hurry. Mother stops him and tells him he's not going anywhere without a good breakfast. She convinces him, pours cereal, son tries it, likes it, and decides to take time to eat. Mother feels great!

• DIRECTIONS

In this one the mother should get to the action of pouring the cereal within, let's say 20 seconds.

-   The mother and son should make their relationship as real as possible.
-   Try not to make the scene argumentative. The mother convinces the son in

a positive way, for instance:

"It'll only take a couple of minutes."

"You need a good breakfast", etc.

– Make your actions as clear and specific as possible.

– As the son, to slow down your cross through the kitchen, you could grab some juice and/or give mom a kiss goodbye. At this point the mom starts to persuade the son to sit down and eat for a minute.

– After the son finally eats and likes it, mom, to get your attention back to the box you could pat it a couple of times and say something like,

"I'm glad I finally found something he'll eat."

–OR–

– You could just think the thought while focusing on the product.

– In using the product, make sure the label (even if pretend) is seen by camera.

Work out the action between yourself and the person you're working with. Remember not to drag out the opening where the mother is convincing the son. Keep the improv moving until all the directions are completed. If you don't have a chance to work it out, the mother or father would have to take charge, sit the son down, and get him to eat, remembering that it is a commercial and should be done in a non-threatening, friendly manner.

GENERAL RULES FOR IMPROVS

There is no end to the type of things you may be asked to improvise. Whatever you improvise try to make it clear and decisive, not just rambling on and stepping all over what the other person or people are saying (upstaging). Listen to the others and when you do speak, *say something that feels honest and sincere for the moment.*

The main thing is to have fun, relax, listen and react naturally. If you can't think of anything to do, don't press yourself or get frustrated. Relax and focus on the situation being played and let your creative juices flow. Instead of thinking of what you can't do, make the situation real for yourself, focusing on your character and the other characters around you. This should help you perform in a natural, spontaneous manner. Your creative dialogue exercises you did in Part 1 Page 46, will come in handy in these auditions. Even though you are doing an improv, make sure you include all the directions and actions given you. Be aware of the casting director out of the corner of your eye so that you can see them cueing you for certain actions and giving you the sign to end the improv. They may make a circle with their hand or fingers which means "wrap it up" or "wind it up", or make a horizontal line with their hand or just say "cut", which means to end it.

• LOOKING FOR A LOOK

This is the type of call where you have the least amount of control over the outcome. This kind of commercial requires that you "read" as a type (you look like the type they want) immediately and has little or nothing to do with dialogue or performance.

On the audition, you would get a polaroid taken, do your slate and profile on tape, and then they may ask you to "tell us something about yourself". It is especially important to get as much information from your agent as possible concerning the part you're being seen for. Try to think of any commercials you've seen for that product and the looks they used on them. If your agent gives you a choice of types, naturally go for the one you fit in the best and is the most natural for you.

If you're going for a special character part, get the look together, and the attitude of the character. If you are asked to talk about yourself, try to maintain the attitude of your character while still being natural and interesting.

• "TELL US SOMETHING ABOUT YOURSELF"

When we're nervous, we have a tendency to talk fast and rattle on. So before you start, take a deep cleansing breath then talk at a slow even pace. This also gives you more time to think and better structure your thoughts and sentences. When told to talk a little and show your personality, beware of being silly. Being humorous and expressive is fine, but just running your mouth and saying silly stuff is boring.

Here are some ideas on what you could talk about:

1. Where you're from and how long you've been here.
2. Aside from acting, what else you do.
   - Hobbies you enjoy, sports you're good at.
   - Parenting - whether you're a mother or father and how many kids you have.
   - Another interesting job or project you're working on.
3. Talking shop (talking about the business)
   - A memorable performance you did that they may have seen.
   - A series or film you're doing or have done. (Be careful of mentioning other commercials since clients don't want you to be identified with other products or even their product if you've done one for them before.)
   - A play you've worked on. Any serious actor should have done a play or plays, whereas you may not have done film or TV. This is always good conversation, especially *good* plays.
   - Interesting people with whom you have worked. Actors or people of

accomplishment in other fields.

- Plays you've seen. If a Broadway show is in town and you've seen it, that's good conversation.

- Classes you've taken. Acting, singing, improvisation classes.

4. Places You've Been

- If you've been someplace exciting and learned something new.

- A trip you're planning.

If you're a productive person with goals and you are serious about the acting business, you can find plenty to say about yourself. Be aware of your diction and enunciation. Even though you're being natural, be professional. Sometimes a casting director may interject a question or funny remark based on something you've said, or try to lean your conversation in a different direction. Keep your sense of humor and go along with it.

• THE CALLBACK (CB)

The majority of auditions you go out on will require a callback before you actually get the job. The first call is usually run by the casting director and the callback is run by the director of the commercial, and is also attended by the clients. Some commercials even have a second callback, for which you get paid under union rules. Try to keep your copy in case you do get a callback. If you can't keep it, *(and most casting directors don't want you to take them)* jot the words down right afterwards while the commercial is still fresh in your mind.

REVIEWING: In reviewing and working on a spot for your callback, don't change it too much from your first audition. Just clean it up, practice until you know it well and it flows. Also, practice it with slight attitude changes because often on callbacks a director will ask you to shade your performance one way or another, or ask you to make it more real and simple. Knowing it well doesn't mean it will be stale, but should help you to make the words your own and say them without thinking about them.

CHANGES: Always be prepared for changes in dialogue and action on call-backs. Although you may have worked on the copy, you may have to do something totally different and be expected to perform it just as well. This is the nature of the business. so always get to a callback in enough time to get and work on any changes. Ask the casting director questions such as:

– Do they want the same thing?

– Are there any new directions or attitude changes?

Sometimes they don't know and when you get in the audition, things may still change.

LISTEN TO THE DIRECTOR FIRST MAKING SURE YOU HEAR AND UNDER-STAND ALL OF THE DIRECTIONS: If you have any questions, ask them. Then make quick, intelligent choices. Be careful of sticking your opinion into it, even-though you may think it is illogical, dishonest or unnatural. Your negative opinions will only get in the way of making the material sound natural and believable, and making the necessary adjustments as directed.

Commercials using reactions or improv are also subject to change, like different cues or timing on reactions. So again, listen carefully to the directions given and ask any remaining questions you may have.

• STAY PROFESSIONAL

It does you no good to get defensive and say you were told by someone to play it differently or any such thing. Just relax, listen, and focus on the present. Everything you do and say in a callback on or off camera is undoubtedly seen by someone in the room and may affect your getting the job.

Keep your professional attitude and if there is any socializing, be friendly and keep a sense of humor, but know when to cut it off and get to work. Be very careful of joking about the product since clients usually don't think it's funny.

• WARDROBE ON CALLBACKS

As far as wardrobe is concerned, it doesn't hurt to wear the same thing you had on in the first call, or at least something very similar, unless you're told otherwise by your agent.

• NOT YET

If the client is interested in you but they haven't quite made up their minds your agent may call and tell you that you're –

"On Avail"

Which means that the clients and the director have not made a final decision yet but they are interested in you and they're checking to see if you are available to work on a certain day or days. Always keep your agent posted of any changes in your availability so that they can let the CD know immediately and they can try to work it out.

Sometimes you may be 'on avail' and you still don't get the job. I hate when that happens! They decide to go with someone else. Oh, well, more to come, and at least you will find out in enough time so if you get another job, you can take it.

• BOOKED THE JOB

This means that you have been chosen to do the job and are set to work on a certain day or days. YES!

GENERAL TIPS ON AUDITIONS

Always Go to Get the Job. You go through so much to get there, you owe it to yourself to do your best. Learning to relax, listen, and focus is a big part of your audition technique. Relaxation helps you to stay open and let all your other work show through. Listening and focusing helps keep your attention on your main objective.

It always pays to mentally review your auditions, even the good ones, because obviously in those you made some good choices. Saying "I should have" is not as constructive as saying "I could have" which leads to more positive statements like, "I could have done it this way, so next time in a similar situation I'll be more relaxed and focused and I'll make the better choice or perform better".

If you decide to get depressed and worry about not getting a job, not only does it make you feel bad, but you can carry it over to the next audition. "Oh, I don't know why I'm bothering, I'm not going to get it anyway." Not a good attitude, and a complete waste of time and effort. Love yourself. Be kind to yourself. Tell yourself you did a good job, you did your best. Or if you didn't do your best, review why and work on that.

Your turn will come, keep the faith!

Chapter 3

HOW TO KEEP
DOING THEM

When you do book a job you would want it to go well. You want to be professional and have your performance be at it's best.

Directors and clients remember the good ones, as well as, the "never agains". It's important to establish a good rep so casting directors will want to call you again and directors will want to work with you again.

Getting the job is one feat accomplished, but by no means is your work completed. Doing the job is another. The actual shooting is the one for the money, the time to really shine. This is your pay-off, but like running a race, the last stretch can be the hardest.

Here are some things you should know to help you to do well and better your chances of getting more commercials.

• BE PHYSICALLY READY

You need to be healthy, in good shape and well rested because the hours are often long and tedious, and the lights very hot.

If you're one who likes to celebrate, save it until the job is done, or until you get that first check.

What's next?

• THE WARDROBE CALL

This is where the size sheet comes in. Director, Mark Berndt says that quite often after having spent a lot of pre-production time making phone calls, awaiting confirmation, and the wardrobe person making contact with the talent (you), there is very little time for the actual fitting and necessary shopping. This is why the correct information is so important on the size sheets. The costume designer (wardrobe person) will always call to confirm your sizes. If they have done any preshopping and you have given the wrong information, time is wasted, and people are bothered. So remember the importance of a correct size sheet.

From the phone number on the size sheet, the costume designer makes contact with you, and asks you, seemingly, to bring everything you own to a fitting in a couple of hours. If you're lucky, you get a day to prepare.

First of all, you don't have to bring your entire closet. Pick out the clothes you feel can really work and are presentable, so you give the designer a couple of good choices. There have been times when I've taken a bunch of stuff and the costume designer never looked at one piece. But then again, there are other times when they did choose one of my pieces, so do your part, but the final decision is theirs.

If they choose your wardrobe, there is a place on your contract to mark it and get compensation for it.

Another thing to consider, but not a requirement, is to have the same look on your wardrobe call as you had on the audition, so once they fit you, they can get the right overall picture. You don't want to shock or confuse them by looking totally different from the person they cast in the spot.

BE PROFESSIONAL

Get all the details:

1.   **Know the correct date or dates that you work and mark them in your datebook**. If it's a weather permit call, which means they'll shoot if the weather is suitable, you may end up shooting on that date or the day or days following that date.

2.   **Know exactly where the commercial is being shot**. If it's a sound stage – know the address of the lot and the number of the stage. i.e. Stage 1, Stage 2 etc.

If it's being shot on location, get a map and/or directions which you completely understand before the day you shoot. Usually they are given to you at the wardrobe call. When you receive them, read through them right away and clear up any questions you may have.

3. **BE ON TIME**

Figure out your travel time based on distance and traffic at that hour, and plan to arrive <u>at least</u> 15 minutes prior to your call. Being late is bad news. Actors have not been rehired because they were late and cost the production company money.

4. **If you're driving, fill up the tank** the day before and get parking instructions. If using public transportation have your **fare ready and your route planned**.

5. **Prepare yourself for your comfort on the set**.

I have frozen my buns off doing a summer shot when the weather was more like winter.

If you're going to be out in the elements bring along extra undergarments or cut off long johns that'll fit under your wardrobe. (See picture pg.124)

If you anticipate that the ground may be damp, especially on these early morning calls, wear some thicker soled shoes so your feet won't freeze.

Bring a big coat to keep yourself warm between shots.

Of course on those hot days try to stay cool, stay out of the sun and drink lots of water. Bring something to keep you occupied while you're not working.

– OR –

When working with other actors watch them perform to help you learn what to do and not to do.

6. **Be Cooperative**

All the people you're working with have been hired to combine their talents to do a job. Working in a positive, cooperative spirit only helps to make the accomplish-

KEEPING WARM: This is a picture of a Toyota spot I did in San Francisco. It was freezing. The white things hanging under my coat are my long johns rolled up.

ment of this feat that much easier.

People react to you based on your action. Try to keep a calm manner and give off good vibes. Even if you get a little nervous or tense, take deep breaths, think positive, and work through it.

Days on the set can be long and tedious, but remember that this is what you're being paid for, and if the commercial runs well, you will continue to be paid for it long after the job is done.

7. Check in With the AD

When you arrive on set, find the AD (Assistant Director) and let him know you're there. During the day make sure he/she, or the 2nd AD, knows your whereabouts whenever you leave the set.

It's not good if they have to go looking for you.

If you need something while you're on set, you can always ask someone to get it for you. There's a PA (Production Assistant) around just for this purpose. But remember, watch the attitude. They are there to assist you not to be abused by you.

8. KNOW YOUR COPY

You need to know your copy inside out and be able to add or take off seconds. Even though they still may change the dialogue, know it well enough so that you can do it without thinking about it.

BEHAVIOR ON THE SET

• CONSERVE YOUR ENERGY

As I said before, the days may be long, the lights you work under are hot. You need most of your energy to give a good performance, so minimize the socializing. Stay on top of the situation. Don't contribute or get involved in any petty mess going on around you. If attitudes start flying, stay quiet and keep a good thought so it will pass you by. Even if it is directed toward you unnecessarily, keep on top of it with a professional attitude and do your best.

• **YOUR RELATIONSHIP WITH THE DIRECTOR**

– All of your direction concerning your performance should come only from the director. They can be male or female, but for now we'll say 'he'. When he is talking to you, listen intently and absorb as much as you can. Any direction that may seem difficult or unnatural, rehearse it and work it out so that you give him what he wants.

– Directors assume their actors are professional, and that they know basically what they are supposed to do. They also assume that you will be able to repeat your performance at performance level as many times as necessary. Don't expect them to hold your hand and guide you along. If you have questions, ask them, but try to take charge of your performance and help the director by giving him one less problem to deal with.

– Don't take directions from clients, other actors, a busy body, or someone who just looks important. If you are approached by someone else concerning your performance and it conflicts or changes something the director has given you, go to the director and clear it up with him since he is the only one that you answer to. He deals with the clients and producers for you.

– Problems?

If you ever feel you are being asked to do something you shouldn't, or there is something you have a problem with that does not go along with your contract, ask to call your agent and clear it up before you go on.

– Suggestions

If you have a suggestion or feel as if you have a way of making something work better, talk it over with your director. Don't be surprised if you're not able to do it, since there are so many other considerations that a director has, which you may not be aware of. Then there are times when you can contribute and create something that was not thought of, but works well in the situation. So don't be afraid to make suggestions, but don't be overly sensitive about them.

TECHNICALLY SPEAKING

As we have discussed, commercials are very technical. Most of your direction may have little to do with your artistic choices, but everything to do with timing, hitting marks and staying in or out of the light. You may have to repeat a performance numerous times and it may even seem like the director is picking on you personally, when the problem is something technical. If you are responsible and you are not hitting your mark or staying in your light and coming in on cue, then the sooner you pull yourself together and make the correction, the sooner he will be able to make a couple of good takes and move on.

• TIMING

Timing is essential in the filming of a commercial. You can do a wonderful take with great interpretation and action, but if it is too long or more unlikely too short, then the take is no good. So the work you've done in shaving seconds off, knowing your copy, and breathing correctly on your phrasing, helps you to feel and know where and how you can pick up your tempo or slow it down to do the take on time. Internalizing, along with diaphragm control, highly contributes to your ability to make the copy work and sound natural in a minimal time frame.

Another important aspect of timing in filming is picking up your cues without overlapping someone else's lines. Unless otherwise directed, the lines of each person need to be separated for sound, so that they can cut away clean and clear when they edit the commercial. So listen and be aware of not stepping on someone else's line, but being able to come right in once they've finished.

• BEATS

These are mentally counted seconds before a cue. A director will often tell you to "wait two beats before entering", "count three beats before you say your line", etc. This means that you basically count 2 or 3 seconds in your head before your cue or action. Usually these are approximated, and your rhythm may be slightly different from his, so it is always subject to change. Sometimes, listening for a cue and counting a certain number of beats coincide, so whether you have to change the number of beats for yourself or speed up or slow down an action to meet the cue, is for you to determine and work out so that you have the right rhythm the director wants.

• 'CUT'

Continue your action and stay in character until the director says 'cut'. Don't assume that once you've stopped speaking, the filming is over. Hold! You can ruin a take by breaking too soon.

• HITTING YOUR MARKS

When you're on a shoot and working with the actual props and sets and you're given a mark to hit, they are crucial. (See pictures Pg. 129) Make mental notes and give yourself visual guidelines so that you hit that mark each time. Line your mark up with something stationary or between two points that you'll be able to see.

BURRELL ADVERTISING INC.
20 N. Michigan Avenue
Chicago, Illinois 60602
(312) 443-8600

CLIENT: Procter & Gamble Company
PRODUCT: Tartar Control Crest
LENGTH: :30 PGCB0903
TITLE: "Sassy Receptionist"

(SFX)

RECEPTIONIST: Honey, it's hard to convince me of anything.

So, when more of the dentists and hygienists here recommended Tartar Control Crest for fighting tartar, I said, hmph -- convince me.

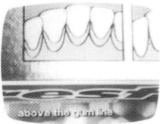

They said

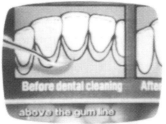

once ugly tartar's scraped away (scrape -- scrape)

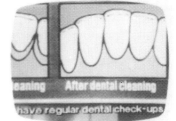

Tartar Control Crest helps keep it away between cleanings.

I tried it

and mmmm --

my teeth feel clean and smooth.

Of course it fights cavities. I mean the name is Crest.

But I won't try to convince you. See for yourself.

ANNCR (VO): Tartar Control Crest with fluoride. The dentist's choice for fighting tartar.

HITTING YOUR MARKS: Notice how the product is set, and how it stays there throughout the shots. I used my chin, and the way my arm rested on the table as guidelines to hitting and maintaining my mark.

When you're directed to walk and stop at a certain point, it is marked on the floor for you. So that you won't have to keep looking at the floor while approaching the mark, try to line it up with something on your eye level, or where you've been directed to look until you get a feel for where it is you're supposed to be. This way, if you need to, you can glance at your mark for verification but you won't have to depend on it.

There are several reasons for hitting marks:

proper focusing of the camera

proper lighting

proper spacing

Failure to hit your marks can result in a lot of energy consuming "takes", so the quicker you master this, the better.

• FINDING YOUR LIGHT

This is a technique that comes from experience, but I can explain to you what it means. Once your light is set (the one that shines on your face) be careful not to move in and out of it during your performance. With experience, you will be able to feel it on your face. It is bright and warm like the sun, but not quite as intense. Find where your light is while working, and what your limitations are in movement. Also, be aware that you're not shadowing your face or blocking someone else's light. The gaffer (lighting director) or the director will make you aware of where you cast unwanted shadows, so make mental notes of it and practice adjusting your movements so that you don't make mistakes. Once they tell you, they expect you to remember.

• CHEATING TO CAMERA

We talked about this technique in Part II during auditions, but it is especially important during filming. When you are to relate to others in the scene, seemingly unaware of the camera's presence, as a professional actor, you should always be aware of where the camera is (unless otherwise directed). Be aware of directing your activity and dialogue in favor of the camera's eye so that your action is seen by the camera and you do not upstage yourself.

Example: If you're talking to someone to the side of you, instead of looking directly at them, let your eyes go to them, but keep your face angled toward the camera. Sometimes the director will even suggest that you don't really even look at the person, but 'cheat the look' and just look in their general directions. The cheat is not noticed by the camera's eye.

Illustration:

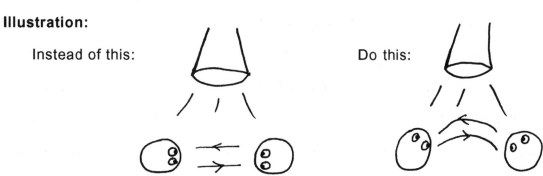

You may also be asked to cheat the product to camera. The same principal applies. Angle the product towards the camera's eye. Any marks you've been given should coincide with this move.

• EATING

When filming a commercial requiring you to eat, you have to consume much more than at the audition. Remember to take smaller bites that look large, and if they cut away in time, you can always ask to spit it out instead of swallowing. In between takes, drink lots of water to help clear your palate and flush out your system so you won't get sick. If you have accepted the job, then you have agreed to eat what is required so make sure you can handle it before you commit. Also, have a light lunch if you know you're going to have to eat again while filming after lunch.

• WORKING WITH CHILDREN

The majority of children you work with don't understand their responsibilities as professionals. They get tired and distracted very easily. Gather all your patience together and work with them to help them stay calm and focused. There is always a tutor and/or social worker on set to tend to their needs and protect their rights, so this is not your job. But if you have to perform with them, whatever you can do to keep them interested and happy would only help you both.

However, be careful not to interfere with directions or distract them while the director is talking to them. If you have time and think it is necessary, work out your business or dialogue with them on the side in a fun, pretend way. Whatever you do, try to remain friendly with them, at least until the job is over. It also helps not to wear them out by playing too much while waiting. Remember the main objective is to keep them calm and focused.

YOUR PERFORMANCE

• REPETITION

If an effort to get the right 'feel' the director wants for the spot, all the moves correct, and the timing exact, you may have to repeat your performance, what may seem like a hundred times.

Don't be surprised, get agitated, or robot-like.

Often times you won't know why you have to do it again. Just try to give the same performance with the same energy and freshness as the first one, unless of course, you're directed otherwise.

If your performance becomes robotic, then it will be difficult to add colors or make adjustments.

So when asked to do it again, forget that you've done it 50 times already. Just go for it like it's your first time through <u>creatively</u> but <u>technically</u> remembering all the directions.

• BE CREATIVE

The more relaxed and focused you are, the more creative you can be. Often times, once they get what they want, they will ask you to do something different. Trust yourself, open up, and don't be afraid to try different things. You'll be surprised what kind of genius can come out of you, if you have confidence, and are relaxed enough to let the creative juices flow. This doesn't mean take it all the way out and start doing strange things, but it does mean coloring your performance with different attitudes and inflections, while remaining focused, internalizing your creative choices, and working them in so that your performance is still within the time frame of the spot.

• MAKING MISTAKES

If you mess up during a take, don't start cursing yourself out or apologizing over and over. **EXCUSE YOURSELF, COLLECT YOURSELF, THEN CORRECT YOUR-SELF**. Even if you joke about it, remember that you still have to correct it, and put it straight in your mind before you go on. Be aware that it is more difficult to say a line correctly when you've flubbed it on the previous take. Pause a few seconds to clean it up. If it is a problem with dialogue, repeat it several times and straighten it out before you say you're ready to go on. It's okay, people make mistakes all the time, so don't be hard on yourself, and at the same time, work on it so it won't take forever to correct it.

• LORD, WHEN WILL WE GET THRU?!

When the day drags on and it seems like they don't know what they're doing and you wonder if you'll ever go home again, just remember you're probably making great overtime for the day, and after the shoot is over, your job is finished and you can soon collect residuals. That should help ease the pain.

• STAY READY

After you've done your first commercial, you should be proud of yourself, but don't stop working on yourself. Keep practicing. Stay toned up and ready. There's a lot of competition out there and lots of people want the same jobs, so make sure your tools stay sharp. You've got to keep your body, speech, and performance ability in tone.

• STAY IN TOUCH WITH YOUR AGENCY

Visit them now and then so they can see you and be reminded of your wonderful self and any changes in you. Also, you get to see their faces, establish closer relationships, and meet any new people working there. Be friends with your agents, and stay in touch with them, keeping them abreast of all address and phone number changes, too.

The more auditions and commercials you do, the more experience you will have and knowledge you will gain. Keep these two points in mind:

* Accept, correct, and learn from your mistakes.
* Recognize, diagnose, and grow from your experiences.

Chapter 4

PRINT

Print is that part of commercial advertising which involves the commercial photography you see in **magazines**, on **posters**, and **billboards**.

If you desire to do print, see if your agency has a print department or find one that does. They will let you know when to get a composite or zed card done (page 140 - 141). As I said, zed cards are mostly used for high fashion, which also comes under print but, in addition include *test* photo sessions, fashion ads, catalog and runway.

As a print model you get paid an hourly rate or a flat daily rate and no residuals. The pay is good but it does vary among models based on experience and demand. Find out from your agent what their current starting rates are. The commission you pay an agent on print is higher than on commercials and that too varies. Make sure you also know your agents policies on time sheets and pay procedures.

As of now there is no union for print, so there are no standard union contracts. Some agents do require you to sign one, which they themselves draw up. Read it carefully and have an attorney review it before signing.

Aside from high fashion catalogues, **print** uses real looking people and character types for product ads.

• PREPARATION

Pictures: You can use a single 8 x 10 shot to get started(see examples pg. 138) but later you may be asked to do an 8 x 10 or a zed card (about 6" x 8-1/2" in size) with 2 or more different looks (see example pg. 139) You may even need to have a 4–sided folded card with some color shots on there which are expensive, so take

Van Elliott

**This could be used for print to get Van started.
He's my husband, by the way. Not bad, huh?!**

SUNDE JOHNSON

L.A. TALENT

L.A. TALENT • 8335 SUNSET BLVD., LOS ANGELES, CA 90069 • (213) 656-3722 • FAX (213) 650-4272

PAPER CHASE PRINTING INC. 213/874-2300

This is my daughter's 8 x 10 with 2 different looks on one side.

Julian Ramirez

This composite could be used for commercials, print and fashion.

This is a 4–sided zed card that is folded.
(Outside)

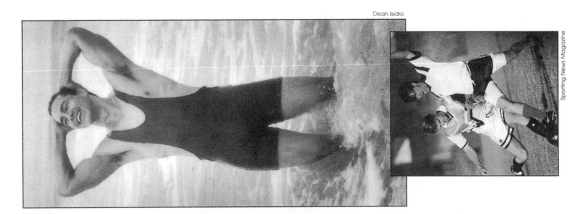

Dean Isidro

Sporting News Magazine

Mitch Burmeister

Jorge Quiroz

Don Lewis

Don Lewis

Lands End

(Inside)

your time, find a good photographer and have a well planned, thorough session. The looks you choose will depend on your type and the kinds of things you will be sent out for.

Portfolios: Once you do a photo session for the composite or zed card, the prints of your different looks that you and your agent choose should go into your portfolio or book. Once you start doing jobs, collect copies of them and put them into your portfolio too. This is not required for print as much as it is for high fashion. Often it's not looked at, but it's a good thing to have to show your experience.

The Call: Most of the time they just want a look, and your agent should be able to tell you what that look is. Here again, as in commercial auditions, get as much information as possible about the location of the call or 'go see', and the type you're being seen for.

Make Up: If it's for real looking people, there's no need for heavy make-up. Be natural looking and make sure it's smooth and you tone down the shine.

• THE 'GO SEE'

This is what a print audition is often called. On a 'go see' always bring along a picture or composite and portfolio, if you have one.

Polaroid: There is NO COPY in print but the polaroid you take on a 'go see' is very important. It should be

VERY EXPRESSIVE

ANIMATED

With Lots of Energy Behind The Eyes

A photograph freezes time and what we see is what you are thinking and feeling at the moment. Because it is still, you need to project lots of energy to give the picture some life.

There are times when you will get some direction as to what they want you to be thinking or feeling in the picture. You have to LISTEN, FOCUS, and EXPRESS yourself with your EYES, FACE and BODY LANGUAGE.

This does not mean making faces, but having real internal thoughts, positive thoughts, about the product or relating to the action you're playing.

If you're not given a specific direction for the polaroid, all you can do is relax, think a good thought, and give a nice smile with expressive eyes.

If you know that it is going to be a very animated ad, make the smile and eyes a little brighter, but not too much. You don't want to distort your face.

If you have to use props try to make your holding positions seem natural.

• THE SHOOT

Even though it is still photography the job is, not at all, easy. You may take a couple of hundred pictures or more during the session and each one should have life.

It is easy for your face to become stiff and your motions stilted.

To Stay Fresh:

—   Shake out and do some stretches between shots.

—   Use your facial exercises to loosen up your face.

—   Blow out between your lips on BRRR.

—   Do some natural moves between shots then relax into your holding positions.

There is a lot of repetition in print work and if you start to feel like you're pushing it, ask the photographer for a short break.

When you finish don't forget to:

—   Fill out your time sheet and have it signed.

—   Collect all of your belongings.

—   Find out when and where the ad will be shown, so that you can get a copy for your portfolio.

So for print work you have to **have energy, be animated, and like taking pictures**.

VOICE OVERS (VO)

Voice Overs include the voices you hear on radio spots, over TV commercials, and cartoon characters. I have worked in all these areas and I love doing them because you can do your job, have big fun and get paid without getting all dressed up or made-up.

You can usually tell if you have voice over potential by listening to yourself on tape and/or by comments and encouragement from your agent or others who feel you have a great speaking voice. There are different categories of voice overs and you can fit into one or more of them according to your voice quality and flexibility.

1. **Announcer**: A rich, rounded, smooth tone with excellent articulation and breath control. Some announcers' voices are very soft and some are stronger with more resonance. In any case it must be very clear and have a pleasant sound.

2. **Character**: These voices are a little unusual, high, or they just may have more color in them. They may be husky, high pitched, or very nasal. Some people have these voices naturally, and some can develop and affect these different qualities.

3. **Animated**: These are for cartoon or animated characters and are mostly contrived voices. They are full of personality, color, and are very distinct. Anyone of us can do an animated voice, through our imagination and creativity. But an important aspect of animation is not only being able to create a voice but also able to maintain and recall it when necessary. Your character's voice has to be consistent throughout the job and recreated on subsequent jobs.

A master of this technique, of course, was the late, great Mel Blanc. I was fortunate enough to work with him and hear him expertly perform several different voices in one cartoon. And, check this, instead of going through the script doing one voice at a time, he would do the entire script, performing each character as they came up. He made instant character and voice changes and remained consistent with each one. It was something to hear and respect.

The Voice Over (VO) industry is a very tight business, and a difficult field to break into. It is almost impossible to get a voice over without representation, and all the good VO jobs are union jobs done under AFTRA (American Federation of Radio and Television Artists).

To prepare yourself for Voice Over work:

- Tape record yourself reading ads from magazines using different announcer and character voices. Then listen to yourself, correcting any nicks in your voice, and keeping check on enunciation, inflections, and breath control. Since the microphone will be very close to you while recording, you should not hear yourself take a breath between phrases. So you have to really use that diaphragm and let the air drop in, instead of gasping.

- Be especially aware of two consonants. 's' and 'p'. Don't hiss the 's's or pop the 'p's.

- Use background music. This helps in putting different colors and levels in the voice and mellowing the sound. You can even practice radio announcing and disc–jockeying using music.

- Create and develop some animated voices. You can come up with different sounds by holding your tongue and lips in certain positions and/or by making dramatic changes in your voice pitch.

- Test your ability to maintain each voice and recreate it at a later time.

Record different voices then go back later and try to repeat them. If you can't remember what you were doing, use your tape to review.

These exercises help you to:

- Make your voice flexible.
- Become familiar with your different voice tones.
- Realize what it takes to maintain and recall different voices.

• VO AGENT

See if your commercial agent has a voice department or get a list of voice over agents from AFTRA. An agent can send you out on voice over auditions based on their belief in your ability or they may have you do a DEMO TAPE and advise you on putting one together.

• DEMO

This is a professionally done tape, with a variety of your voices, that represents your abilities as a VO artist.

- They are sent out to casting directors who, in turn, may call for you to audition or may just cast you from the tape.
- The people who put these together for you are found in trade advertisements or your agent can refer you.

  Before making the investment, check out their work, listen to some demos they've done and compare prices.

  They should have lots of different copy and background music to help you put together a professional tape. Use the work you've done at home to give you some ideas.

• 'J' CARDS, ETC.

It is up to you how much you're willing to invest based on your desire, your pocketbook, and your potential as a VO artist.

In addition to the actual cost of the demo tape production, there are additional costs for: reproductions of the tape, printing of 'J' cards (which go inside the cassette jacket with your name, voice qualifications, agent info, and your picture on it, if you wish), and mailings to advertising agencies and casting directors.

• WORKSHOPS

There are reputable voice over workshops that you can join to develop your voice talents. They can also help to network you into the business. The majority of VO workshops are taught by producers and casting directors in the VO industry. If you're good, the word can get out and you can begin to work quickly. It all depends on you.

Of course you don't have to join a workshop. You can do as I have done, work on yourself.

I'd like to thank Don Pitts, my VO agent for some information included in this chapter, also Mary Lynn Wissner who helped me put together a great demo tape.

SURVIVAL TIPS

• KEEPING YOUR HEAD TOGETHER

Because you want to do commercials, or you need the money or both, you'll want just about every job you're up for. In most cases, you're going to feel that you should have gotten a particular job because you felt you were so right and/or did a great audition. If you don't hear anything from those auditions, you could suffer some very annoying feelings; injustice, rejection, resentment, self-doubt, confusion, or just ticked–off. Don't put yourself through it. You never know what's on those peoples minds. You, in fact may have done a great job, but there may be other factors over which you have no control.

When I talked to Beth Holmes, a known CD on the West Coast, she stated, "You do a great audition, the CD's eyes light up, but you just thank them, walk out, and wash your hands of it." They may have changed the type, you didn't look like the child's mother, etc. Whatever the reason, it most likely has nothing to do with your performance. Megan, another CD, says, "You may look too familiar to them, you may remind the client of their secretary, someone they know and pass right by you."

Remember also that one of the main things that determine whether you get the job or not is your ability to read as a "type" in the first 2 to 3 seconds. This means that when they view you on tape you must immediately look like the type they want. There are also times when one can bring something special to an audition and give the director and client a new and different way of seeing it. So don't worry about it and don't put yourself through unnecessary stress over auditions.

• YOUR NERVES

As soon as you can change back into your normal comfortable stuff, and wash that make-up off your face (girls) do so. After an audition, your job is done. Changing back to your normal self helps to release any stress concerning the audition and encourages you to move on to the next thing. Just treat each one as a seed sown. Keep the faith, keep at it and they'll start sprouting one by one.

• CARING FOR OUR BODIES

Your body is your main tool, and young or old we function best when we are healthy and in tone. Younger people are more active, or at least they should be, and they get their exercise through their normal daily activities. Their health is up to their parents or guardians, and their health habits are developed from their upbringing and environment.

As we get older and become responsible for ourselves and others, it is up to us to have the knowledge, will, and the discipline to care for, and maintain our bodies so that they function at their best and don't readily succumb to disease and the ailments of aging. Since most of our daily lives don't require the use of our bodies in such a way as to strengthen them, we need to find ways to add caring for ourselves as part of our daily routine. We should be continously searching for ways to keep strong that go along with, and fit into our lifestyle, so that maintaining a healthy body becomes part of how we live.

In my forty-five years I have been exposed to and experienced many methods of exercise and caring for my body; dancing, martial arts, aerobics, working out in the gym, yoga, running, and walking. I've found them all to be very beneficial, and whenever I get the chance, I do one or the other, and relish it. But being a wife, mother of two, actress,writer, teacher and whatever else I'm called to do, that chance doesn't come often. So in order to maintain a functional level of energy and keep my body looking good for my good-looking husband, (and my profession) I have created my own system of exercising whenever, however, and wherever possible, using what I've learned together with what I feel. I'd like to share it with you and open you up to a new way of "using what ya got". [Please be advised that before you start any exercise program, you should consult a physician].

• MIRROR, MIRROR...

In our discussion about commercials, we started by looking in the mirror and that is how we will start here. Go to a full length mirror and take a good honest look at yourself in your normal posture, stance, and state of being. Notice the overall energy you project, if any, and the spots or areas where you hold tension in your body; the strong areas, the weak ones, and be honest about what needs improvement.

– Are there areas of the face that are tense?

– Do you frown?

– Do you hold tension in your jaw?

– Is your mouth pulled down on the sides or poked out?

– Do you grit your teeth?

• YOUR POSTURE

– Are you holding tension in your shoulders, arms, or hands?

– Is your chest caved in or held up?

– Is your stomach area strong and calm or weak and nervous, or just too darn big?

– Are you standing on good, strong pulled up legs or something less in various degrees?

– Is that derriere nice and firm or is it just hanging around back there?

From looking at myself and others, and from good ballet training, I've realized the importance of good posture. It helps you to look better and feel better by letting the energy flow properly throughout your body and giving your organs proper room to function. If the chest is caved in or depressed, it must be lifted. Hold up the rib cage to give the organs space. Guys have an easier time with this since they are naturally stronger in the chest. If you look at body builders, male or female, their chests are always lifted because it's so strong. Once you lift the chest and press the shoulders down you'll notice a lot of facial tension will disappear.

Good posture will also give your center of energy room to function properly. As you pull the stomach in, be aware of the diaphragm expanding and releasing. Feel the strength in your legs by pressing down into the floor with the whole foot (heels through the toes) and pulling up in the knees. If you squeeze the inside thigh muscles together, the buttocks will automatically tighten and you'll have a nice firm basis to stand on. To get the pressure out of the back and pull the neck up straight and long, imagine a string being attached to the top of your head pulling you straight up into the air. As you're being pulled up, you resist by pressing the heels into the floor.

Now let's have a quick posture check:

1. Stomach is held in, supporting the diaphragm. Strong center.

2. Head is pulled up.

3. Shoulders pressed down.

4. Chest lifted.

5. Arms relaxed.

6. Inner thighs tight.

7. Knees pulled up.

8. Feet pressed through the floor.

9. Rib cage lifted up out of back.

10. Face is relaxed and pleasant looking.

Don't we look better!

Check your posture often. If we aren't used to holding our bodies in this manner, making these adjustments may seem strange, but we can see and feel the immediate benefits. An important note to remember is that once you have completed an exercise, maintain good posture and just breathe into it instead of collapsing. This will help reshape the body habits into a better form. Our body is an amazing instrument. Just as it heals itself and performs well, it can also hold a lot of tension, stress, congestion, or blockage which results in pain, infection, and disease. So we have to work to release these things and let the blood and energy circulate, through stretching, exercise, and massage.

• KEEPING IN TONE

Now in order to maintain a sense of strength and well being, let's do some simple, convenient toning and stretching. We'll talk about massage later.

Review the face, eye, neck, and shoulder exercises that I gave you in Part 1. Remember to repeat them until your muscles get very tired, that way you will actually be strengthening them. In addition, here is a good one for clearing and strengthening the nasal passages. With the poor air quality in some of our major cities we need the help.

Using the thumb and pinky finger of the right hand, holding the other three down, inhale.

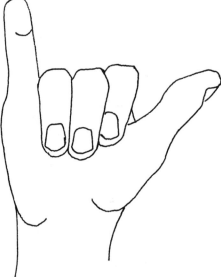

Now hold the right nostril closed with thumb, exhale through the left nostril slowly. Then slowly inhale through the same one then close it (the left) with pinky and release the thumb and exhale through the right nostril slowly, then inhale into the same. Repeat this several times. Not only does this help clear and strengthen nasal passages especially with a cold or sinus problems, but it also helps to calm you if you're feeling nervous or tense.

Review the warm-up exercises in Pt. 1, and add them to your daily routine along with the following. Work on all of them at different times and become more familiar with your body so that keeping it toned becomes just a part of the things you do. I won't give you a set number of times to do the exercises because each person's ability may be different. Just repeat them until you really feel it, and add a little more each time. Don't limit yourself to certain places to do the exercises. Continuously find other places and times where and when you can care for your main tool. Don't be shy. Make it part of your life. If you really believe you can do them, you can. At least you will do more than you decided on the negative side.

Just relax into them. Don't think of them as being hard or horrible, but great and revitalizing! Feel your body strengthening, working out the knots and supplying it's needs, since we need our bodies so much.

STANDING

• HEAD TILT

This one is to strengthen and keep the neck flexible. In a squatting position, feet apart, your hands are out in 2nd position or resting on knees. The head is tilted forward, now turn it to the side, looking to the farthest point behind your head, then the other way. Maintain a nice slow steady pace and really twist the neck.

Now up and down. Head goes down pressing the chin into the chest then all the way back, using the back of the neck to lift the head, strengthening your neck muscles and stretching the front of the neck. Keep facial muscles relaxed.

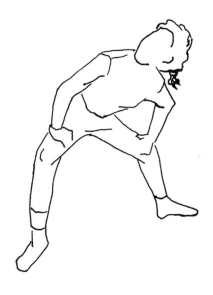

• BACK HEAD TILT

Now stand up. This one works better with arms out in 2nd position with the feet apart. Tilt the top of the body back reaching out and slightly forward with the arms for balance. Turn the head to each side looking down at the farthest point behind the head on the floor.

Make sure the neck stays stretched out during the exercise to develop long stretched out muscles, not tight bulky ones. For an extra stretch of the neck, standing up, with your right hand, pull the top of the head toward the right and with the left hand pull the shoulder down. Change sides.

While you're in the standing position, do the **head rotation** and the **neck and shoulder exercises** mentioned in Part 1. Also review the side stretches for the waist and the deep leg bends in second position for the legs, hips, and derriere. Starting with the arms out in second position as you plié (go down) pressing knees out, raise your arms over you head until they meet, keeping the shoulders pressed down, then straighten the legs and arms circle down. Repeat...

Still Standing – For *feet*, *ankles*, and *legs* – do some relevés (pushing up to the balls of feet) in second position since you're there from the above exercise, and then in first position, heels together, toes out

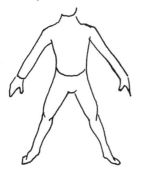 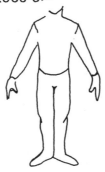 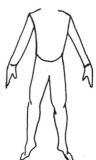

These can be done anywhere; waiting in line, at the sink, waiting for a bus, or if you need more balance, use a counter, sink, desk, back of couch, or chair, etc.

Here's another simple one with great results for feet. As you stand, grab the floor with your toes. Spread your toes apart, then try to dig them into the floor in a gripping motion. This is especially good for those of us with flat feet, weak arches, or just stiff underdeveloped feet.

Now while you're standing on the set and need some revitalizing or a little lift, squeeze the inside thigh muscles together like you're holding a million dollar bill in there, and pull up in the diaphragm, or as we've been calling it,

(your center). As you breathe in, fill up the back first, expanding it and lifting up through the top of the head. Doing this gives you a stronger posture and a better energy flow. This, like many of the others, is an anytime, anyplace adjustment.

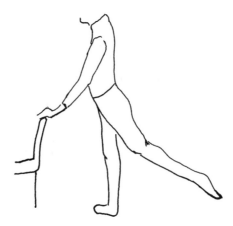

• NOW FOR THE DERRIERE

For the derriere, back of legs, and back, still standing using an edge for balance, lift a straight leg up behind you with a pointed foot. Keeping the chest lifted, shoulders pressed down, energy coming from your center (area around the diaphragm). Lift the leg up as high as you can without tilting forward, then place it down gently, barely touching the floor with a pointed toe. Do it enough on both sides so that you really feel it, as with all the exercises. Using your center for support, really tighten that derriere and point the whole foot, even lifting the little toe more so that the outside of the foot works too.

To stretch out the back, feet together, both hands on the counter, bend over to a flat back, keeping the arms and legs straight. Really stretch the back out from the hips.

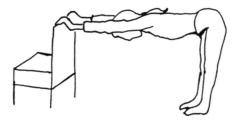

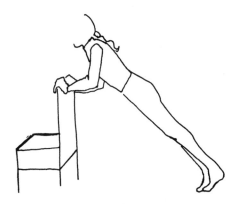

While we're here, let's do some **push-ups** using the same edge or padded steps. These will build the arms, chest, and back for good posture. Guys, who are more advanced, can do these on the floor. Stand away from the counter so that you get a good lean. If you're using the steps, do it on a different step each time to change levels and work different areas. Also using a counter or steps, do the exercise with your hands at various widths apart.

Use the whole flat part of the hands with wrists bent, so that they stay flexible and strong. Okay, body as flat as a board, using your center of energy to pull everything together and tight, chest up, shoulders pressed down, push away, then lower. Your body should be rigid, energy coming from your center which is pulled up and firm. Feet should alternate from being flat to a relevé (lifted), but keep them close together. Exhale as you push up, inhale as you lower. Go at a nice, even pace, changing your position slightly after you've tired in the other.

Do the counter stretch with flat back, and arms and legs straight to release it. In this position, bend one knee at a time. This stretches out the shoulder blades, and back of the legs. Really stick the butt out and pull the back out of the hips.

Stair steps are a great place to stretch the legs and hips.

Placing one foot at the edge of various step levels, press down with hips facing front, each side getting a good hip and inside leg stretch. Now pull back into a straight leg position, head down, but pulling the back out of the hips. This is a good stretch for the back of the legs. Relax into it.

SITTING

There are even some things we can do to help our bodies while we're sitting in a car, or at the office, or just sitting and waiting. Whenever or wherever you're sitting, you can give yourself a **posture and energy lift** by using the image of the string at the top of the head, lifting up and pulling in your center, pressing the shoulders down and squeezing the buttocks together. Press your weight into the chair, letting the back rest into the chair and the feet rest on the floor.

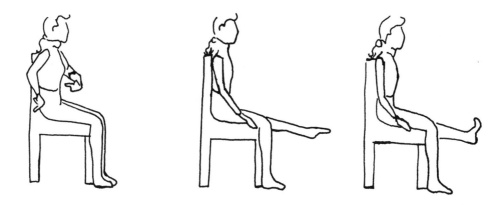

These are minor adjustments to make, but they are so helpful and you should do it whenever you think about it. This is an especially good posture to assume while eating, giving the digestive system room to work correctly.

If you have room to straighten your legs, lift them up and let them down slowly, keeping your knees together with the toes pointed, then flexed. At times, you can hold in the straight position, just feeling the strength in the thighs.

Relaxing the feet, just squeeze the **inside thighs** together.

FOOTWORK

We need our feet so much. Strong healthy feet can really make a difference when standing on set for 14 hours. Even as you walk around, try to use the feet more, keeping them flexible and really feeling the ground beneath you. Spread the toes and let them grip the floor as you move. Now back to our sitting position:

Now lift the heel all the way up until only the tip of your toes touch the floor. Then press the heel back into the floor. Really concentrate on working the heel which will in turn, also work the ankle and instep. On the lift, really press the heel forward. On the release, really press the heel into the floor. If your foot starts to cramp a little, just relax it, then continue to work it slowly, trying to release the tension in it.

Now move your feet away from the chair. Flex them all the way up as high as you can, keeping the toes open and up. Now point the foot, push the instep up and stretch the toes toward the floor with only the very tip touching. Remember not to ball the toes up. Let them point out, sending energy through the floor. Now repeat. Flex–point, flex–point...

• ANKLE CIRCLES

Everything tight and together all the way down -- thighs, knees, calves, ankles, and feet, which are pointed and resting with the tip of the toes on the floor, make circles with the ankles to the left, then right. Even the toes can bend and make circles.

• TOE SQUEEZE

Feet on the floor. Ball the toes up as tight as you can. Now stretch them out as far and wide as possible. Repeat...

Now lift one leg up at a time and **shake the feet out** keeping the ankles really loose and release all the tension in the feet.

You should have been keeping your thighs very tight and knees together during the exercise. Now let's **stretch it out** by opening into second (knees to side) feet on the floor (instep high). Press the knees out with either your hands or your elbows, releasing all the tension in the hips, sending the energy out and down.

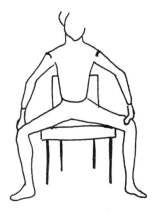 

• FOR THE MIDDLE

Keeping the stomach muscles pulled in flat, lift one knee at a time as high as possible. The knee can go straight up or to the side. Don't arch your back! Use the stomach muscles to pick up the leg and not your back or the upper thigh. Now stretch it out in second position or just sit back and relax.

• FOR THE UPPER BODY

At a desk or table -- In the good posture position with the shoulders pulled down, press the palms of the hands into the edge of the desk, bend and stretch the wrists out and flex the chest muscles.

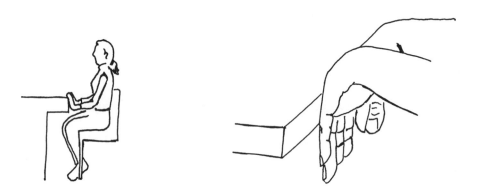

Now bend the wrists the other way with the back of the hand pressed against the edge. Flex the chest muscles. Press the shoulders down, but keep lifted. Without the use of an edge, press the palms of the hands together, flexing the chest muscles. Hold, hold, hold, and repeat.

• HAND SQUEEZE

Arms hanging to your sides, squeeze your hands into tight fists, then stretch them out with the fingers spread wide apart. Repeat. Circle wrists vigorously one way, then the other. Do this exercise with an open relaxed hand, then a tight fist. Really work all the kinks out.

Press the upper arms into the body, keeping the shoulders pressed down, then release.

Repeat several times.

Some of the upper body exercises described can also be done while standing. Become familiar with all of them and even add some variations that you may feel. Pay close attention to what's happening to your body as you work on it. Whenever there is pain or stiffness, work through it by breathing and relaxing into it.

<u>ON THE FLOOR</u>
(Or on a Firm Bed)

Let's start by lying on our stomachs and finish on our backs.

• **BOTTOM SQUEEZE**

For the buttocks and lower back —— Bend the knees with the feet straight up and together. Lift the knees as high as you can (which will probably only be an inch or two). Keeping the feet together, open the knees then squeeze them together. Open-squeeze, open-squeeze. Keep the shoulders relaxed, but concentrate on really bringing the bottom to a point.

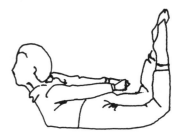

To also work the upper back, hold the head up, and the arms straight behind you with the palms together. Then relax and go into a **counter stretch**, which is to sit back on your heels, head relaxed and down, arms out front. Now relax all those muscles you've just worked and then do the bottom squeeze again.

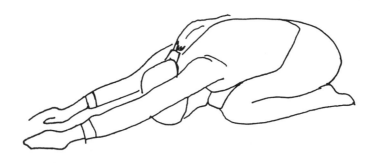

• THE AIRPLANE

For the whole back – Still on your stomach, arms out straight to the sides, legs straight. First lift the legs with toes pointed, buttocks very tight, hips pressed to the floor, upper body relaxed. Hold – Hold!!

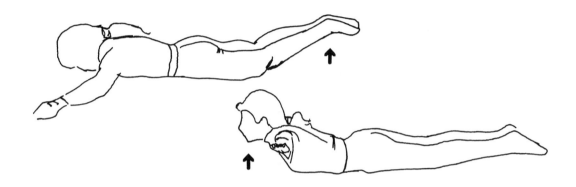

The legs should come up a little higher each time you do it. Now lift the top half. Legs relaxed, chest off the floor, head up, arms up and out like an airplane and hold- hold - hold. Then relax. Now do both ends together and let's fly!!!

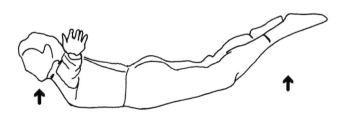

Hold - hold. Then relax and go into the counter-stretch sitting back on your heels.

Another good stretch for the stomach, neck and lower back –– Still on stomach, feet slightly apart, legs straight, palm of your hands on floor under your shoulders. Straighten the arms as much as possible, lifting the chest, head dropped back, – – buttocks, legs, and back relaxed.

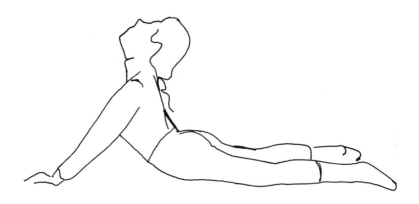

NOW LET'S TURN OVER ON THE BACK

• STOMACH

On your back, hands behind the head, knees up and together. Lift the head and shoulders up into a curl, pushing the back and stomach flat through the floor. Use the hands only to assist a little, not to lift the head. Keep the chin tucked into the chest.

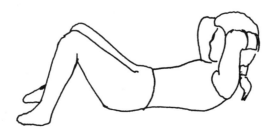

Just lift the head, shoulders, and upper back, then lower. Don't release all the way down. Just lower and lift, lower and lift...

For the **lower part of the stomach**, press the back against the floor, head lifted, with the chin tucked, hands behind the head for just minimal support. Bring your knees up, point the toes and extend one leg at a time to a straight position, but not touching the floor. Now bring that leg back while you extend the other in the same manner. Remember to keep the stomach muscles as flat and pulled in as possible. You don't want to develop muscles that stick out. Don't forget to breathe!!!!!

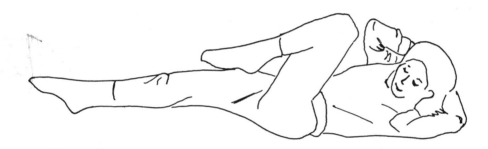

Do these leg bends until you just can't do them anymore, then relax flat out on the floor, arms extended to the side and just breathe.

PRESS AND STRETCH

This can be done at any time, especially upon waking up to help stimulate you and get the body in line.

Lying flat, **press yourself** into the bed (or floor) starting with the heels go up the body, legs, hips, back, arms, neck, and head. Then release and stretch out the arms and legs extending them to opposite ends of the room. Relax and repeat.

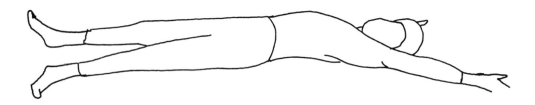

• BREATHING

Breathing is very important throughout all these exercises. The general rule is that you exhale while you're exerting the most energy, and inhale on the release. You should follow this rule on the slower exercises, but for the quicker ones, just breathe at a normal rate, fully and deeply. Whatever you do, don't hold your breath! Holding your breath creates tension and prevents the much needed oxygen from flowing through to your muscles.

To keep your back nice and flexible, let's give it a little stretch. Still on your back, arms out to the sides in second position, palms facing down. Bring the knees up and together, now keeping both shoulders on the floor, bring the knees down to one side, pressing to the floor, and keeping the knees as close to the chest as possible. Now keeping the knees together, twist to the other side, letting the knees go all the way down to the floor.

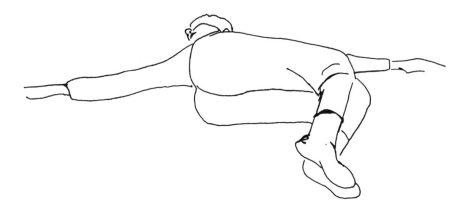

Even the head can go in the opposite direction of the knees, giving you an extra stretch. Really feel the twist in the lower back, breath into it then let it out and try to release any tension or stiffness you feel back there.

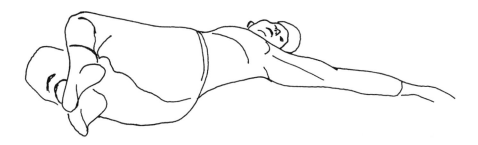

RELAX

Now just lie flat on the floor. Keep your eyes closed and let every muscle in your body go – just melt into the floor. Breathe nice and easy and relax. If you fall asleep for a few minutes... fine. If you have more time, stay down there. This is the best way to relax and let go, if only for a few minutes. If you really let your body go, and just let the thoughts pass through until you doze off for a while, your body will get as much rest as if you had napped for a couple of hours. So if the energy is low, or you just need a break, especially right before an audition, go lie on your bed, or on the floor, flat on your back, making sure you stay warm, and relax a while. It can give you a new energy and maybe a new outlook.

ADDITIONAL STRETCHES

There are many ways of stretching the body. Some I have mentioned already, but whenever and however you feel the need to stretch, do so. If you just listen to your body, along with the stretches you are familiar with, you can improvise others.

• BENDING OVER

I know we have been told to bend our knees to pick up something so that we won't hurt our backs. My feeling is that that ol' back could use some stretching and so could the backs of your legs. As you bend over to pick up something (just the lightweight stuff!!), keep the legs straight, stretching out of the hips, and releasing the back of the legs. If you're really stretched out, you could keep the back straight, instead of rounded as you reach down.

Here's one that is a combination of several, but covers a lot of areas. Start in this position.

Facing sideways, both feet pointed in the same direction, legs apart. (A little further each time). Arms stretched out front and palms together. Everything should be in line facing one way.

①

Drop the head back and using your outstretched arms for balance, lean back, releasing the upper back, and letting the weight of the head take you as far back as possible.

(2)

(3)

With the front leg straight, the upper back gets a stretch. With the front leg bent, the middle and lower back get a stretch. Now straighten up easily, remembering to breathe and using the image of the string pulling you up.

(4)

(5)

• ROLL OVER

Roll over letting the back round slowly, hands reaching all the way down to the floor. Try to keep the body in a straight line, pull up in your center, press the feet into the floor and pull up in the legs for balance. Now roll up slowly letting the head be the last thing to straighten up. Repeat the stretch, starting with dropping the head back. Go as far as you can, straighten up, then go forward. Face the other direction or change feet and repeat. Remember to breathe during the exercise and hold in the forward and back positions for a good stretch.

While you're facing the side, do the lunge stretch, bending one knee at a time and getting as close to the floor as possible.

Keep the heels pressed into the floor to really stretch the back of the legs.

• STRETCH DOWN

Facing front, feet still apart, stretch over and down. Grab behind the ankles and pull through if you can. This can be done along with the side stretches we did in the warmups (Part 1). Now reach over to the right, then left.

• ROUND OVER

Sitting on the floor, legs together. Feet pointed, then flexed, round over letting the head touch the knees.

Besides the rounded back, try this and the next one with a flat back, pulling the chest as close to the thighs as possible.

Still on the floor, legs open in second, relaxing in the hip joint, but pulling up in the stomach and the legs, round over to center, pulling your head to the floor, then over to the right leg, then the left leg.

Here's a good one, but do it slowly and carefully.

Yep! Okay, start with the legs together, sitting up. **Roll back**, lifting your hips up and taking your legs over your head. Be very careful and move slowly and keep your head straight forward. If you can, let your feet touch the floor. Keep your legs straight or bend them, even bend them to the ears and relax.

If you can, **lift the legs straight up**, supporting your back with your hands. Keep your legs very tight, feet pointed and lift up as much as possible. This will relieve pressure from a lot of interesting places.

Using a wall for support, and a pad under your head, standing on your head is great for relieving pressure and improving circulation. Using your hands for balance with your fingers pointed to the wall, lift your legs resting your body against the wall. Make sure you're far enough away from the wall that you'll lean on it and not fall back the other way.

Now that I've got you standing on your head, I guess we can wrap this up. Come down like you should have gotten up. Using your hands for support, bend your knees and lower your feet. Get out of the position slowly so that you won't get dizzy. Now relax.

There are a lot of ways of staying in tone and taking care of yourself. Keep looking for ways to add it to your daily activity, and form some good habits about it. Whenever you can, attend a dance class, do aerobics, martial arts or yoga class, work out at a gym, go walking, running or bicycling, whatever. If you invest in exercise equipment, get a good piece and use it. A **jump rope** is a great inexpensive investment because jumping rope is an excellent and fun way to exercise, especially to music. Swimming is great too, although not my favorite, because I don't want to get my hair wet, and those of you with hair like mine know what I mean.

Anyway, make these exercises and stretches part of your life.

<u>MASSAGING</u>

Another wonderful habit to develop is self-massage or acupressure. Anytime you feel a knot or some tension in your body, use your fingers to apply pressure to it to break it up and send it on it's way. Really feel for the knots and kinks, and press 'em and rub 'em out of there.

There are a lot of nerve endings in your hands and feet, so they need massaging as often as you can do it.

You can even massage your organs and intestines and move gas and wastes around in there so they can be on their way too. Lying flat, feel around your stomach, (upper, middle, and lower), and massage and press it gently, while you stay relaxed and try to break up any congestion or move any blockages to keep things flowing smoothly.

It's good to do this at night, right before sleeping. If you ever get a chance, get some professional acupressure done. It's wonderful for you and they know all the points. It'll also give you a better understanding of how to do it yourself. A note about this is that when you're having it done, if they are pressing too hard, let them know, but try to relax and take as much pressure as possible.

<u>WATER</u>

Drink plenty of this. It's so important. Carry a good size container with you and make sure you finish it at least twice in the day.

<u>BEING SICK</u>

This is one thing a commercial actor does not have time for. You never know when you have to work, so you need to stay well and stay ready to work. So eat the right things, exercise, and keep a 'check' on the partying!

THE FINALE

I could go on and on. Maybe I will in the next book, but we've covered quite a bit in this book. We've learned how to prepare and keep ourselves in a "ready to go get 'em" state. We've learned about our center of energy, our diaphragm, and how to use it to control our energy, our voice, and our emotions. We've learned how to break down copy, how to act on auditions, and how to act on set. We've also learned new words and new ways of living. This, like many other workbooks, should be carried around with you as part of your "stuff," until you become really familiar with it's contents, and your techniques become second nature. Like anything worth having, a successful commercial career takes time to develop. So stay in a positive frame of mind, accepting and learning from your experiences and always looking forward to reaching higher levels professionally and spiritually. Pray a lot, recognize and be thankful for your many blessings and stay focused. Now get to work. God bless you, and see you on the set! !

Glossary

... of words and terms used in the commercial industry

action
> 1. Your Movement within the scene.
> 2. Your cue to perform.

action cue
> The point at which you begin to perform – on the word "action".

AD
> An abbreviation for assistant director. The person you check in with when you arrive on set, and the person who should know your whereabouts at all times on set.

ad
> An abbreviation of advertisement. A photographed advertisement for a product or service.

ad lib
> Speech or action that has not been written or specifically rehearsed.

AFTRA
> American Federation of Television and Radio Artists. A talent union that covers video tape productions, voice overs and radio.

agent
> A person or group of persons that represent talent and are paid a commission. They are responsible for submitting you on jobs and negotiating your contracts. They should be francished by SAG.

audition
> Also known as an "interview" or "call" in which an actor/actress performs before a client in hopes of getting a job. The actor/actress may be required to read lines from a script, do pantomime, improvisation, and in general perform for the purpose of showing his/her qualifications for a role.

beats
> Moments or seconds counted mentally before a cue, or before continuing action.

Book – Booked

A job confirmation.

Callback

A request for a talent to return for an additional audition for the same client and the same job. Those competing for the job have been reduced in number. The actor is paid for the 2nd callback (3rd call in all) and any more thereafter.

Call time

A specified time at which the talent should arrive on set. The call time is usually earlier than the "on set call time" to allow for make-up and wardrobing.

Call sheet

A form specifying what is to be shot and all the personnel and equipment required to film on a certain day.

camera left

The left side from the camera's eye. If you were facing the camera, it would be your right.

camera right

The right side from the camera's eye. If you were facing the camera, it would be your left. [Camera left and right are the opposite of stage left and right.]

case history

The life history you create for your character that coincides with the facts in the play and your relationship to the other characters.

casting director – CD

The person in charge of the casting session, representing the producer, and is responsible for choosing talent to audition for the producer and client.

center

Your center of energy. The area around and including the diaphragm.

character

A reference to the person you represent in the acting situation.

characterization

To give background, life, expression, behavior, colors, and motivation to the person you are portraying in an acting situation.

cheat the look

This term is used so that the camera can get a better picture. Instead of looking directly at someone or something, (which causes you to turn away from camera) you instead look in that general direction but favor the camera's eye more.

cheat to camera

The same explanation as above but not just in reference to a look, but anything in the camera's eye favoring the camera.

client

The person/people who represent the advertising company for which the commercial is being done.

close-up/CU

A very tight shot of a performer or an object, showing more detail.

cold reading

An unrehearsed reading of a script, usually at auditions.

composite

A set of pictures of a talent on one sheet, maybe two sides, with a headshot and several other different looks. It may also contain some talent statistics and the agent's logo.

contact sheet

A photo sheet of usually one roll of film from which you choose the pictures to be enlarged.

copy

The script of a commercial or voice over.

copy breakdown

The analyzing of a script for the purpose of getting it to performance level.

creative dialogue

Speaking, relating a story or event, fact or fiction, and continuing non-stop for any given amount of time.

CU

Close-up.

cue

A verbal or visible signal for you to begin to speak and/or act.

cue cards

Large white cards (approx. 2' x 2-1/2') with the copy printed on it large enough to be read at a distance during an audition.

cut
A verbal or visible cue for the performer to stop speaking and/or acting, given by the director.

cycle
A thirteen week period of time in which a commercial is used or put on hold.

date book
A well-organized, dated book or electronic organizer containing your appointments, auditions, phone numbers, addresses and pertinent information you need for the business.

demo tapes
A variety of commercials or voice over work done in a professional manner that represents your abilities as a artist.

diaphragm
A body partition of muscle separating the chest and abdominal cavity that expands and releases as air goes in and out of the lungs.

directions
Instruction and guidance on the action or conduct of a performer given by a director.

external
A surface performance with no real feeling behind it.

fitting
A scheduled time and place for the talent to be wardrobed for a commercial.

first position
In ballet, a position in which the heels are together, feet turned out, legs are turned out from the hip while squeezing the inside of the thighs together.

first refusal
A client would like to reserve the right to hire or refuse you for a job on a certain day if you are offered another job.

flippers
False teeth for children that are used for cosmetic purposes and easily removed.

focus
To give your full, undivided attention to what you are doing.

frame
The area of vision that is actually seen on TV. This is usually smaller than the camera's vision and marked off in the viewer. (Although, not on your everyday camera)

gaffer
A lighting director or the person who places lighting instruments.

hitting your mark
Stopping your action at a specific point that has been determined by the director.

improv
An abbreviation for improvisation. An unrehearsed performance done on the spur of the moment. (You may be given the overall situation and some direction, but the action and dialogue are unscripted and unrehearsed.)

"J card"
> A title card that fits into a cassette tape holder with your information and agency on it.

law of averages
> A working theory that out of so many attempts to get a job, you will actually book a certain percentage.

mailings
> Packages containing your picture, resumé, and cover letter or announcements of an upcoming performance that is mailed to agents and/or casting directors for either representaiton or showcasing of talent.

manager
> A person who supervises and is responsible for the career of the talent they represent. They work on a commission basis and on a more personal level than an agent.

mark
> 1. An exact place on the floor that the actor must stand on or stop at as directed. It is usually indicated by tape.
> 2. An exact place where a product or object is to be put, or where an action is to take place.

mic
> An abbreviation for microphone.

mime
> The art of acting out a situation or action without words or props.

monologue
> A solo performance by an actor.

MOS
Mit out sound. There is no sound being recorded during filming. (It's from the Germans and it's mit because they couldn't pronounce "with".

motivation
Your reason for saying or doing what you're doing.

MOW
A television movie of the week.

on avail
The client is checking your availability for a certain day, but has made no final decisions.

one liners
An acting assignment that involves a single line or phrase.

on location
A designated place other than a sound stage to film a commercial.

out clause
A clause written into the contract that allows you to get out of the contract if certain terms aren't met.

out of frame
Performance or action that cannot be seen within the television frame.

PA
An abbreviation for production assistant, a person on set who is available to assist you, as talent or the production crew in any way possible.

pantomime
Conveying an object or an action without the use of props.

"P & G Look"
P & G stands for Proctor & Gamble. The look is very 'middle of the road', neat, well groomed, and casual.

pick up cues
> To come in on time with your action or speech.

plié
> In ballet, a movement that involves the bending of the knees in a turned out position as the upper body stays pulled-up and the derriere tucked in.

print
> A photographed advertisement of a person, product, and/or service.

producer
> The creator and/or organizer of the commercial. (Usually in charge of financial matters).

product
> The object or service being advertised.

production company
> The company responsible for the actual making of the commercial.

professional
> One who knows his/her craft and is paid a comparable salary for it.

profile
> A side view of your face and/or body.

program use
> The use of a commercial during an actual program. The product is the sponsor of such program. Talent is paid for each program use.

proofsheet
> See 'CONTACT SHEET'.

props
> Objects which are set or carried in a scene.

repertoire
> A list of dramatic pieces which you can perform.

reproductions
> Professionally made copies of your picture(s) with your name and maybe the agents logo on them.

resumé
> A professional, typed, list of your credits, training, union affiliation, and skills.

"Roll Tape" / "Roll 'em'
> A verbal cue to start recording on tape or exposing film.

SAG
> Screen Actors Guild. Talent union which covers all jobs done on film.

second position
> In ballet, a position where the feet are approximately shoulder length apart and turned out. Second position for the arms is up and out to the sides, slightly rounded at the elbow, (like you're holding a huge ball) with the shoulders pressed down.

sense memory
> Being able to recall and demonstrate the particulars of an object, situation, or condition in it's absence.

set
> 1. A designated area where the commercial is being shot.
> 2. The area of performance including furnishings and props.

shooting
> The actual filming of the commercial.

shot has to match
> This means that the piece that is presently being filmed has to match a previous shot as far as hair, make-up, position of talent, and props on the set.

sign-in sheet
> A form distributed by SAG or AFTRA and provided by the casting director on which the talent signs in on arrival, giving the required information and signs out on departure.

size card / size sheet
> A card or sheet provided by the casting director and filled out by talent on request, giving name, address, phone numbers, measurements, ss#, etc. A polaroid of talent is often stapled to this sheet or card.

slate
> The opening shot taped in an audition where the talent states their name, and if requested, their age and agency.

spot
The commercial being auditioned for, or being filmed.

stepping on lines
Saying your lines before another actor has completed his. Therefore, not leaving space for clear editing.

storyboard
A printed sheet including pictures of the planned shot setups, and the corresponding dialogue for a particular commercial.

take / takes
A ~~completed~~ recorded version of the action and/or dialogue being filmed or taped.

talent
The performer, actor, or actress.

theatrical agent
An agency that represents talent for feature films, television shows, stage plays, movies of the week, etc.

3/4 Shot
Picture showing not just the head but a portion of the body.

tools
The skills and equipment you need to work as a professional in the commercial business.

trades
Publications that deal with the entertainment industry, i.e. Variety, Backstage, Drama-Logue, Hollywood Reporter, etc.

transition
A change in thought, mood, or attitude.

union
An organization that represents talent and protects their rights i.e., SAG, AFTRA, AEA (Actors Equity Association - Theatre)

unit
Each city is given a certain number of units according to it's population. These units are figured in determining your pay for the usage of the commercial.

upstage
1. The area of the stage closer to the back curtain or backdrop.
2. Overshadowing someone else's performance by mugging, stepping on lines, or messing up direction. (Not a nice thing to do)

voice over
Off camera dialogue, radio spots, voices of cartoon characters.

wardrobe call
A designated time and place for the talent to be fitted in the wardrobe to be worn in the commercial.

weather permits
If the weather is favorable the commercial will be shot.

wildspot use
Usage of a commercial broadcast by non-interconnected single situations, a use that is independent of any program or is used on local participating programs.

"Wind it up" / "Wrap it up"
A visual or verbal cue to bring dialogue and action to a finish.

work permit (entertainment)
A legal document issued by the state granting a minor permission to work.

wrap
Refers to the completion of work on a particular set, sequence, or location.

xylophone
A musical instrument. Has nothing to do with this book.

X
Your mark. Where you should stand, stop, look, place an object, etc.

Yes
The preferred answer to the question, "Did I book the job?"

"Zed card"
A smaller composite geared more toward fashion.

1974 CLIO AWARDS
FOR ADVERTISING EXCELLENCE, WORLDWIDE

In recognition of outstanding advertising, this certificate is awarded to finalists and winners of the 1974 CLIO Awards competition.

Finalists and winners were selected from more than 3,800 entries worldwide by over 450 advertising/marketing creative professionals from 14 countries, meeting as judges in more than 100 sessions in eight countries on four continents.

Finalists and winners were announced during "CLIO Awards Festival Week", proclaimed by the Mayor of the City of New York.

U.S. and International Advertising Awards Presentations took place at the following events:

Annual CLIO Print Luncheon, Plaza Hotel, June 11th.
Annual CLIO Radio Luncheon, Plaza Hotel, June 13th.
15th Annual CLIO Television/Cinema Awards Ball,
   New York Hilton, June 14th.

More than 2,200 advertising professionals and guests from all over the world attended "CLIO Week" events, designed to provide "the greatest week in the world for advertising". Among the events were daily exhibits and showings of outstanding Print and Television/Cinema Advertising, the Association of National Advertisers/Radio Advertising Bureau's one-day Workshop, the aforementioned Presentations, and a television production of a 90-minute segment of the CLIO Awards Ball.

The CLIO Awards worldwide celebration of advertising excellence continues year 'round with hundreds of meetings, showings, seminars and other events involving many millions of people, as well as the advertising professionals whose varied talents and skills are thus recognized and acclaimed.

Paul Foley
Paul Foley
Chairman, CLIO Awards Advisory Board

Bill Evans
Bill Evans
Director, CLIO Awards

Television
CLIO WINNER: TOYS/GAMES
Tonka Toys - "Excuses"

Agency: Carl Ally, NY
Production: Horn-Griner, NY
Details: Film, 30 Seconds, Color
First Telecast: October 1973
Client Supervisor: Robert Moeller
Account Supervisor: Allan Faecher
Copy: Dave Altschiller
Art Director: Ted Shaine
Agency Producer: Bob Schenkel
Producer: Irwin Kramer
Director/Cameraman: Steve Horn
Editor: Jerry Kleppel
Music Director: Susan Hamilton
Music Composer: Dick Behrke
Casting Director: Chris Raugh
Actor: Vernee Watson ←(Me)
Voice Over: Murray Hamilton